iMac
M4
USER GUIDE

Comprehensive Beginner Seniors
Manual to Setup, Use and Master
the 2024 Mac Desktop with M4 chip
plus Tips & Tricks on macOS
Sequoia and Apple Intelligence

Leandro Barnes

TABLE OF CONTENTS

CHAPTER 15: MANAGING WINDOWS 214

CHAPTER 16: TAKING SCREENSHOTS OR SCREEN RECORDINGS ON AN IMAC

CHAPTER 1: IMAC M4: A FRESH PERSPECTIVE

The new iMac, powered by the game-changing M4 chip, is a manifestation of Apple's commitment to tucking power, elegance, and performance into one neat package. This variant is targeted at users desirous of top-of-the-line performance wrapped in a colorful ultra-slim profile.

SPECS

Let's take a closer look at each of the highlighted features of the iMac M4:

1) M4 CHIP: UNPARALLELED PERFORMANCE FOR EVERY TASK

Underneath it all is an Apple M4 chip. M4 chip redefines the all-in-one desktop, with a quantum leap forward in speed and responsiveness for iMac. For everyday tasks, the iMac with M4 delivers up to

1.7 times faster performance compared to its predecessor with the M1 chip. That translates into as much as 2.1 times more performance for more intensive work, like photo editing and gaming power for work and play. Further, the Neural Engine within the M4 chip makes this iMac ideal for AI workflows, leveraging maximum benefit for Apple Intelligence.

2) APPLE INTELLIGENCE: REVOLUTIONIZING USER INTERACTION

The M4 iMac is designed for Apple Intelligence, representing the next level in personal intelligence at the company. It introduces innovative ways users will interact with a computer to evolve workflows, communication, and self-expression. It's designed to keep users' privacy and security front and center while offering intuitive, transformative capabilities. This AI-driven experience makes the iMac among the most intelligent and privacy-conscience all-in-one desktops on the market today.

3) PLETHORA OF VIBRANT COLORS

Available in a gorgeous array of colors, the new iMac lets users pick one that fits their style and workspace. In supplement, these options are given by the ultra-thin, minimalist design element in the iMac, something that has come to define the way Apple approaches product aesthetic sensibilities. Sleek profiles and vibrant colors make the iMac an absolutely gorgeous addition to any setting, with modern design adding a touch of personal flair.

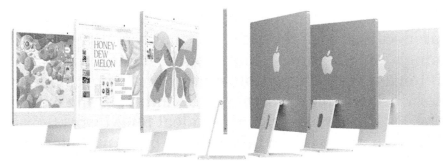

4) NANO-TEXTURE GLASS DISPLAY OPTION

Apple has given users reason to be clear of view and comfortable with the introduction of a nano-texture glass display option on the iMac. It cuts glare, improves visibility, especially in bright environments, while maintaining the same spectacular visuals of the Retina display. It already has a 24-inch 4.5K Retina display, which is praised by many because of its crystal-like sharpness and color accuracy-mandatory for media professionals, creatives, or really anybody who wants the best images. That gets further refined with the Nano-texture option, which cuts down on reflections so one can have a comfortable viewing experience without compromising on image quality.

5) UPGRADED 12MP CENTER STAGE CAMERA WITH DESK VIEW

From enhanced video calls to content creation, upgrade to the new 12MP Center Stage camera with Desk View-a unique capability made possible by advanced software that delivers a dynamic, wide-angle view. Desk View is great for presentations, demos, and even working with someone; it captures the area surrounding the user while keeping them centered. This camera taps into the power of the M4 chip to process images in real-time and give users clear, high-quality visuals even in less-than-ideal lighting.

6) ENHANCED THUNDERBOLT 4 CONNECTIVITY

M4 iMac is designed to have up to four Thunderbolt 4 ports, which would make high-speed data transfer and multiple peripherals hooked into it possible. The most important factor connected with this feature is its ability to connect external monitors, storage, and a number of other accessories via Thunderbolt 4 at incomparable speed and dependability. Each of these supports data transmission, charging, and video output all in one go, thereby making the iMac literally all-purpose in terms of handling the external connections.

7) SLEEK AND DRAMATIC DESIGN

Apple's iconic, slim iMac design is retained, and the M4-powered variant keeps an exceptionally thin profile. Since powerful internals are fitted within this iMac, it remains one of the most efficient in desk space and among the lightest in its category. As such, this design makes the setup seamless and will beautifully integrate into any workspace without flouting its performance.

8) COLOR-MATCHED USB-C ACCESSORIES

Apple's attention to detail really comes full circle with the new color-matched USB-C accessories accompanying this iMac. Other than adding to the aesthetic coherence of the setup, these accessories also afford users high-performance and ergonomically designed tools that match the vibrant color scheme of their iMac. This holistic approach to design and functionality pushes the refinement level of the overall iMac experience.

9) AFFORDABILITY AND ACCESSIBILITY
With prices starting at RM5,799, this iMac is quite a steal, considering the powerful specs thrown into it, further complemented by unified memory and other premium features. The inclusion of 16GB of unified memory on the base model will have the machine well-equipped for light and heavy applications alike, thus offering a robust computing experience out of the box.

10) IMAC IN THE BUSINESS SPACE
Sleek in design, high on performance, the iMac has been a popular machine in professional circles. However, with its M4 chip and color choices, the new iMac could be your best fit within storefronts and client-facing areas where technology and good looks combine for a memorable customer experience. Highlighting powerful hardware with beautiful design, iMacs can be face-forward, attractive workstations in boutiques, studios, and showrooms.

11) VERSATILITY FOR DIFFERENT USERS:
It's universally appealing in its versatility: for families, students, creatives, and business owners alike. Robust performance, a competitive camera system, and aesthetically customizable experiences are just a few of the things it avails. Whether for productivity or entertainment, the iMac M4 can fit in any environment or purpose, letting users work both efficiently and enjoyably. In itself, that allows for huge adaptability- really an ideal device for a massive audience because of how it enables usability tailored to satisfy the diverse needs of millions.

POWERED BY M4 CHIP

The iMac M4 unlocks an unbelievable leap in power, performance, and capability, courtesy of its powerful M4 chip. A deep dive into how the new processor will lift the experience:

1. ENHANCED CPU PERFORMANCE

At the heart of the M4 chip is an advanced CPU, which executes tasks with unmatched efficiency. Powered by what Apple claims is the currently "world's fastest CPU core," the chip M4 offers as much as 1.7x faster performance compared to the M1-carrying iMac. This, in fact, translates most visibly into non-intensive usage-patterns such as multitasking, application switching, and web browsing. You can easily jump between several apps, do high-level searches, and open multiple browser tabs in Safari without slowdowns. That makes daily interactions with the iMac a lot smoother, more responsive, and more delightful.

2. POWERFUL GPU WITH ADVANCED GRAPHICS ARCHITECTURE

Going beyond the CPU, the GPU of the M4 chip has been overhauled to incorporate Apple's most advanced graphics architecture to date. That means it's up to 2.1 times faster than the iMac M1 and is especially ideal for creatives and gamers. Editing photos gets significantly quicker with the M4, as the chip flies through high-resolution images with even the most complex edits. Gaming receives huge strides courtesy of graphics-heavy games like Civilization VII for smooth playing and immersive experiences. It's all possible because this powerhouse GPU enables fluid graphics rendering, realistic textures, and a high frame rate that drives demanding visual experiences on the 4.5K Retina display.

3. UNIFIED MEMORY FOR SPEED AND EFFICIENCY

The new M4 iMac features 16GB of unified memory standard, upgradable to a maximum of 32GB for those power users who need more. The high-bandwidth memory improves multitasking and general performance. The M4 chip itself features unified memory that is shared by both the CPU and GPU, so access to data is faster, and resources can be shared more efficiently. This naturally leads to a better user experience: apps spring out of their states faster and more smoothly, and that, in turn, makes working with computationally heavy tasks such as video editing, 3D rendering, or big projects with data way easier.

4. A FASTER NEURAL ENGINE FOR AI AND MACHINE LEARNING

Perhaps one of the most notable features of the M4 chip is its improved Neural Engine, which is more than three times faster than what was used in the M1 iMac. That makes iMac M4 the most powerful all-in-one desktop for AI-driven tasks. Besides, this advanced machine learning of the Neural Engine enables users to automate intelligently, understand photos, and predict text more quickly than before. Realistically translating this into efficiency for a user-from photo curation to photo sorting in image libraries and real-time language translation. Thanks to this Apple Neural Engine, the AI enhancements make the workflow seamless across a lot of applications-from creative to enterprise-class. That makes it a force for a productivity powerhouse in itself.

5. HOLISTIC PERFORMANCE BOOST ACROSS ACTIVITIES The M4 iMac has been designed to make each and every aspect feel faster and more efficient. Be it an instant response of launching the app, reduced latency in complex workflows, or the ability to handle GPU-intensive tasks-the M4 chip boosts every feature of performance. For creative pros and gamers alike, or productivity aficionados, the new iMac M4 gives an experience that keeps pace with one's needs, arguably making this one of the most capable and versatile desktops available today.

6. BETTER PRODUCTIVITY FOR FAMILIES, SMALL BUSINESSES, AND ENTREPRENEURS
Powering the iMac M4 is up to 1.7x faster performance in key applications, including Microsoft Excel, than the M1 model does. This leap in speed turns how users work with spreadsheets, organize data, and perform analysis, taking on complex calculations and working with huge data sets. On the other hand, web browsing in Safari is also faster by as much as 1.5x, so you are sure working-researching, shopping, or collaborating with others online-is easier. For families and small business owners, smoothly switching to other apps and managing workflow much quicker than before will ensure everyday productivity is amazingly efficient.

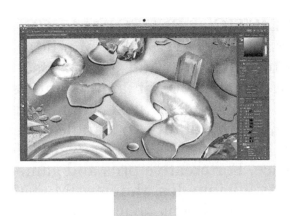

7. SMOOTH, HIGH-FRAME-RATE GAMING EXPERIENCE

The iMac M4 will allow gamers to exploit its powerful GPU in all its glory, which allows frame rates to be as high as twice those in the preceding M1 model. When running more graphically oriented games like Civilization VII, users will see very smooth and responsive performance, with much higher frame rates, making gameplay far more visually appealing. The leap in graphics performance gives way to smoother motion, sharper detail, and true-to-life color on the 4.5K Retina display. It makes the iMac M4 capable of handling resource-intensive programs with ease and also a decent gaming machine.

8. UNMATCHED PERFORMANCE FOR CONTENT CREATORS

Content creation just got a lot more efficient with advancements in photo and video editing on the iMac M4. That is, editing in demanding applications like

Adobe Photoshop picture editing app and Adobe Premiere Pro video editing app is up to 2.1x faster when compared to the iMac M1, important upgrades to tasks featuring complex filters, multi-layered effects, and high-resolution media files. This will further enable the user to work on edits of intricacy without having to wait for render times and thereby see their creative changes in real time. Creatives will be able to work even more smoothly and do more in much less time, positioning the iMac M4 as a serious option both for photographers, videographers, and graphic designers alike.

9. COMPARISON WITH LEADING INTEL-BASED SYSTEMS

Apple's M4 iMac leaves the competition far behind. Against the latest Intel Core i7-equipped 24-inch all-in-one PCs, the M4 iMac is up to 4.5x faster. It's a performance leap, thanks to the M4 chip's efficiency and tight integration with iMac hardware, which lets it blow through tasks and applications far quicker than most traditional Intel setups. In practice, that means a faster, more responsive experience across the board, from boot times into application launches and task completion.

Besides that, the new iMac M4 is up to six times faster when compared to the top-of-line Intel-based iMac. This powerful shift of Apple Silicon in the iMac product line rounds off such a leap to ensure users benefit from a modern, high-speed computing experience that maximizes their productivity, creativity, and entertainment.

10. OPTIMIZED MULTITASKING AND WORKFLOW EFFICIENCY

Conquering multi-tasking across several applications with ease, the M4 iMac boasts what Apple claims as the world's number 1 (currently) fastest CPU core. Thanks to the speedier core, users will seamlessly flip between Safari and Excel among other apps, with no lag or delay in sight. Regardless of whether users are doing research, trying to wrap up a spreadsheet, or organizing files, users get the very same fast response times that make it easier to manage tasks and streamline workflows efficiently.

11. UNPARALLELED GRAPHICS FOR GAMING AND CREATIVE APPLICATIONS

The M4 iMac is fitted with a GPU especially for graphics-intensive tasks; hence, it will provide a smooth and quality experience for gamers and creatives alike. Gamers playing highly anticipated games such as Civilization VII will enjoy the fluidity of high frame rates and exceptional detail bringing every scene to life. The advanced GPU in the iMac M4 allows creators to apply complex effects in a flash and make high-resolution edits with apps like Photoshop and Premiere Pro. It's all about an improved GPU architecture that has given a serious visual boost. Be it gaming or working on creative projects, the iMac

M4 gets the job done with surprising precision and power.

DESIGN

The newly release iMac M4 has a stunning palette of colors that speaks volumes of modernity and injects a personality into any workspace or living space. Each color is painstakingly prepared by Apple to bring out an individualistic personality in the iMac, balancing well between a bold expression and subtle elegance. Let us look at some design and functional features that come with these fresh color options:

1. SEVEN COLORS OF VIBRANT APPEAL

The latest avatar of Apple's iMac is made with one of seven hues: green, purple, blue, and classic silver, yellow, orange and pink. Each color has been crafted to speak volumes, liberating you to choose a shade that best personifies your persona or sets off your surroundings. From bright to toned shades, from energetic to cool-everything is just right in this range of colors.

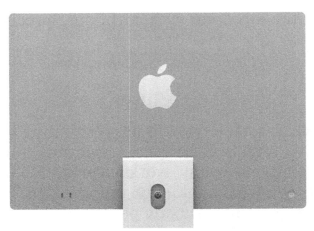

2. DYNAMIC DUAL-TONE DESIGN

The iMac comes in dynamic, bold colors at the back, while the front is reserved with softer, much-subdued tones. Such a split design is functional and aesthetic. The bold colors making a visual impact on the back are viewable when one has placed their iMac on an open space or hooked to the wall where it's the focus; simply, they stand out. Meanwhile, the front of the iMac is softer in tone to create a calmer, more focused enclosure that minimizes distractions and promotes productivity.

3. COLOR-MATCHED ACCESSORIES FOR A UNIFIED LOOK

Every iMac now comes with a color-matched Magic Keyboard, Magic Mouse, or optional Magic Trackpad, making it easier than ever to keep things nice and consistent in look. This is reflected even in the accessories themselves, which match the color of the iMac. The design will ensure that workspaces feel unified and thoughtfully designed, whether users choose blue, orange, or any other color.

4. USB-C INTEGRATION ACROSS ACCESSORIES

The iMac's Magic accessories like Keyboard, Mouse, and Trackpad have now shifted to USB-C from the previous Lightning connectors. This will further facilitate charging and connectivity, as now all their Apple accessories can be charged with a single universal USB-C cable. But this move to USB-C is one considerate inclusion that speaks not only of Apple's commitment to future-proofing its technology but also to industry-standardizing this space for easy charging and connectivity of the iMac's accessories with other USB-C-capable devices.

5. STYLISH AND UTILITARIAN COLOR CHOICES FOR ANY ENVIRONMENT

The colors are to feel at home in everything from professional environments to creative spaces and home offices. The sophisticated silver model exudes timeless charm for minimalistic ensembles, while purple and blue shades introduce an air of sophistication. For those that like a fun and playful feel, colors like orange and yellow fill the room with liveliness. Every color is considerately chosen to increase the aesthetic appeal of the thing without being too overpowering for the user's space. Here, iMac has become stylish and practically forward desk centerpiece wherever it may be placed.

6. FURTHER PERSONALIZATION AND SELF-EXPRESSION

Even the new color options provide a more profound level of customization and expression. From striking to low-key, one can choose whichever suits their vibe and gives character to their setup. Since its beginning, iMac has been an all-in-one desktop for daily tasks and creative endeavors alike. These new colors make it even easier for users to feel connected to their devices in a way that reflects their style and preferences.

DISPLAY

It gets even better with the Nano-texture display option and the advanced 12MP Centre Stage camera on the iMac M4, which raise the bar even higher in display quality and video call capability, making the system highly versatile for professional and personal use. Key Features include:

NANO-TEXTURE DISPLAY OPTION
1) Unparalleled Clarity on a 24-inch 4.5K Retina Display: The 2024 iMac has a massive 24-inch display with each revision continuing to raise the bar with its sharpness, vivid reproduction of color, and intricate detail clarity. Today, Apple ups the ante on the premium display with an option in nano-texture glass for added depth.
2) Reduced Reflections and Glare for Optimal Viewing: Specially engineered to be as low-reflectivity as possible, the nano-texture glass reduces glare and reflections so that the screen is more legible in highly illuminated environments. And this opens up new possibilities in iMac placement, making it practical for sunny environments like a bright living room or even a storefront where ambient light could interfere with the view. A nano-texture layer reduces glare and reflections without compromising brightness or color vibrancy.

3) Improved Visual Comfort in various Light Frames: Glass nano-texture for users who often work or game in different lighting conditions minimizes eye strain and provides a clearer, more comfortable view. Whether it is for office work under fluorescent lights or on bright sunlight, this feature gives clarity without the usual distractions from glare and reflections, providing views from nearly all angles.

AMPLIFIED VIDEO CALLS WITH 12MP CENTRE STAGE CAMERA

1) High-Resolution Centre Stage Camera: With the main idea of video calling, the iMac M4 has fitted an upgraded front camera. Giving video calls a higher resolution that keeps you sharp and clear from any distance through FaceTime or Zoom among others. It boasts a much larger pixel sensor than earlier models to capture more light and detail than ever before, making it good for both business and personal calls.

2) Centre Stage for Seamless Framing: Centre Stage is actually an intelligent framing feature that involves the camera using its wide-angle lens to automatically track subjects and keep them centred in the frame as they move. Great for families wanting to be in-frame together on video calls, or presenters needing to move around while not being out of frame, Centre Stage adjusts seamlessly and unobtrusively, creating a far more

dynamic and engaging experience for all participants in a call.

3) Desk View for Versatile Presentation Capabilities: Desk View follows through with the unique capability of capturing both the user and their desktop using the camera's wide-angle lens. This will be ideal for educators walking through a lesson, creators showing a project, or even professionals presenting documents and objects on video calls. Desk View takes the iMac M4 a notch further in making it a remote presentation tool, giving top-down visuals without requiring any additional equipment.

4) Studio-quality audio to match the visuals: The iMac M4 completes this with a studio-quality, microphone system that is tuned to produce imposing clarity and noise reduction through beamforming so that voices can come through loud and clear. This way, one is assured of seamless remote collaboration without cuts. Further paired with an immersive six-speaker sound system boasting balanced bass and treble, the iMac M4 presents an all-in-one A/V experience-to compare with dedicated video conferencing equipment.

CONNECTIVITY

The latest iMac M4 comes equipped with a higher degree of connectivity to further the wheel of versatility, productivity, and security, making it a powerhouse for professional and personal usage.

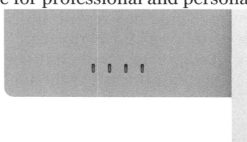

1. FOUR USB-C PORTS WITH THUNDERBOLT 4 SUPPORT

1) Unmatched Transfer Speed: This is enabled because all four USB-C ports on iMac M4 support Thunderbolt 4 for extremely high-speed data transfer at speeds as high as 40Gbps. This allows users to connect a raft of high-speed accessories like external SSDs, docks, and high-resolution monitors, with the ability to seamlessly integrate additional storage, multimedia, and charging docks into one streamlined workspace.

2) Dual 6K Display Support for Expanded Workspaces: Compatibility with Thunderbolt 4 further enables the iMac M4 to support connections to as many as two 6K external displays for an increased digital workspace-a pretty important advantage for some users. By combining the iMac's own dazzling 4.5K Retina display with two more high-resolution monitors, the user can extend their visual field to more than 50 million pixels. This setup is highly valuable for

content creators, graphic designers, and other professionals needing more screen space to multitask in complicated ways, photo editing, and video production.

3) Integration with Streaming Peripheral: It includes four USB-C ports, and this means that iMac M4 will easily accommodate all the useful devices without any additional adapters or converters. From memory card readers and external hard drives for greater storage capacity to graphics tablets and audio interfaces, users can easily attach everything to make setup easier and their workflows smoother and faster.

2. WI-FI 6E AND BLUETOOTH 5.3 FOR ADVANCED WIRELESS CONNECTIVITY

1) Next Generation Wi-Fi 6E: The iMac M4 gets Wi-Fi 6E for faster and more stable internet connections, even in networks. Wi-Fi 6E takes advantage of the 6GHz band to extend latency and bandwidth farther. For this reason, it is more suitable for flawless high-definition streaming, massive file downloads, and online gaming. Because of all this wireless efficiency, it will assuredly be a seamless experience-from users collaborating in video conferencing, transferring big media files, to simple web browsing with multiple pages opened.

2) Enhanced Bluetooth 5.3 Connectivity: Bluetooth 5.3 addition will make the iMac M4 more connected with peripherals like wireless

headphones, keyboards, and mice in terms of stability and interference. This version supports faster data transfer and better efficiency of the battery to keep all user devices reliably paired, whether a person is working from across the room or engaging in high-bandwidth activities like gaming or the creation of multimedia.

3. TOUCH ID INTEGRATION - SECURE AND CONVENIENT

1) Fast, Safe Authentication: With Touch ID on iMac M4, security and ease of access go hand in hand. This feature provides an unprecedented level of flexibility in unlocking the device for users, as they are able to switch it on using their fingerprint for fast, safe authentication. This will make starting work faster and secure because users spend less time typing passwords, hence data protection against intrusion is guaranteed.

2) Apple Pay and Purchases in the App Store: It also allows the facility of online transactions securely through using Apple Pay and making purchases easily without calling for further authentications. Similarly, applications from App Store may be installed easily with never-before speed, allowing immediate authorization via Touch ID.

3) Fast User Switching: Touch ID allows multiple users to share one iMac because of its Fast User Switching feature. Whichever users have their profiles and settings on the iMac can easily log in with just a tap of their finger onto the sensor. This

makes it very useful in shared facilities, such as homes and offices. The transitions among the different user environments can now be seamless without any compromise on privacy or personalization.

MACOS SEQUOIA

The iMac M4, running macOS Sequoia, is polished and engaging, with comprehensive features aimed at productivity, gaming, organization, and increased integration with other Apple devices. Below are some detailed specifics about major features macOS Sequoia brings to the iMac M4, for instance:

IPHONE MIRRORING FOR SEAMLESS DEVICE INTEGRATION

1) Seamless transitions across devices: It means work can be done directly on the iMac screen with the iPhone Mirroring on iMac M4. Because of that huge integration, one is able to reply to messages that come, see notifications, and even open applications from the iPhone right on the iMac. It all turns into one big workspace where it becomes difficult to tell where the Mac ends and the iPhone begins.

2) Smoothened Workflows by Access to Apps and Notifications: They can handle tasks on either of the two, like checking schedules, responding to texts, or even managing calls right from their iMac without having to toggle between devices. This is

pretty useful for professionals and multitaskers alike, as activities are consolidated and easier to flow between desktop and mobile tasks .

IMPROVEMENTS TO SAFARI: HIGHLIGHTS, REDESIGNED READER, AND DISTRACTION CONTROL

1) Highlights for quick access to the main information: The new Highlights feature in Safari instantly pulls the most relevant information from web pages, saving users time when they are looking for specific data-whether they are researching, shopping, or reading news. This functionality optimizes the information retrieval process, making browsing more efficient.

2) Smart Reader Mode with Table of Contents and Summaries: The overhauled Reader Mode now includes a table of contents plus advanced-level summaries for easier navigation through long articles or verbose pages. This would be perfect for researchers, students, and avid readers who need to access and make sense of a lot of information in relatively little time.

3) Focus Your Browsing with Distraction Control: It adds Distraction Control, enabling the user to mask distracting elements on web pages, including ads, notifications, or parts of the page. This makes it very helpful in focused reading for work-related research by allowing users to take greater control over their browsing environment to better suit their needs of focus.

ENHANCED GAMING WITH PERSONALIZED SPATIAL AUDIO AND GAME MODE

1) Personalized Spatial Audio: Spatial Audio offers added immersion to game playing, with audio smitten to the preference of each user and head-tracking for an all-encompassing audio experience. It adds an added layer of depth that makes game worlds feel real with soundscapes richer and directed in a manner that best fits on-screen actions.

2) Improved Game Mode: The Game Mode optimizes the system resources, including CPU and GPU, for gaming applications, allowing smoother frame rates and lower latency. With this feature added besides the strong performance of the M4 chip, it makes iMac one of the most engaging gaming platforms, particularly with anticipated releases like Assassin's Creed Shadows, wherein visual enhancements and smooth gameplay contribute to the player's experience.

BETTER WINDOW TILING FOR ORGANIZATIONAL CONTROL

1) Efficient Multi-App Workflows: Window tiling in macOS Sequoia has been redesigned to make switching between and organizing open applications easier. You can have windows side by side, stack them on top of each other, or choose

the preferred layout that best suits your needs for multitasking. It is an essential tool for professionals when many apps need to be opened and visible all at once-be it designers working in Photoshop next to reference material or business users comparing Excel sheets.

ALL-NEW PASSWORDS APP FOR SECURE CREDENTIAL MANAGEMENT

2) Centralized Access to Credentials: The new Passwords app is going to securely store all credentials, including passwords, passkeys, and other sensitive information in one place for easy access by users in managing their digital security. This tool will be quite helpful for those who have to manage many accounts, because it makes logging in easier across devices and websites.

3) Integration with Passkeys: With passkey support added, the Passwords app future-proofs user credentials by migrating to the latest security standard that skips traditional passwords for added security while interacting online.

PERSONALIZATION FOR VIDEO CALLS

Improved Virtual Background Options: macOS Sequoia also brings a set of new backgrounds that include color gradients and vibrant system wallpapers for video calls. These will be useful for users to bring personal touches into the surroundings in a video call. Adding their personal photos is an option too, and one can make calls to friends, family, or other colleagues quite appealing. They've given an aesthetic appeal to video calls.

It's these virtual background options that add a level of professionalism to the calls by adding an aesthetic consistency that makes video calls polished and put together. That's a feature valuable in personal and professional use and versatile enough for any situation or preference.

APPLE INTELLIGENCE

Apple Intelligence in the iMac M4 is an energetic quanta of personal computing. This is a new paradigm of features and functionalities where intelligent and adaptive functionalities are modeled while fully bearing in mind user privacy and security. Aspects that relate to what Apple Intelligence is, how it works, benefits to the users, and its impact on the consumer experience in the iMac M4 are aspects we shall look into below but in detail. Detail

PERSONAL INTELLIGENCE INTEGRATION

1) Reimagining User Interaction: Apple Intelligence essentially turns personal intelligence into a simple computing task to make the iMac M4 more intuitive and responsive to the needs of its user. It uses machine learning and AI to predict users' behaviors, preferences, and work patterns with the intent of changing responses and functionalities. This is because personalized ways ensure efficacy and satisfaction wherein the

system can predict needs and streamline workflows. This means:

2) Custom User Experience: Apple Intelligence analyzes how users interact with apps to optimize system performance, including offering suggestions of useful tools or actions that might be available, and personalized recommendations. For example, if the user very often edits photos, the operating system may show quick access to image editing software or offer enhancements, based on previous photo edits, to simplify the creative process in question.

POWER OF APPLE SILICON AND NEURAL ENGINE

1) High-Performance Computing: iMac M4 harnesses the full capabilities of Apple silicon and the innovative Neural Engine, which enables blazing-fast execution and quick performance for complex computations. Architecturally, it's designed to run AI and machine learning workloads on-device, greatly improving responsiveness and lowering latency in apps. Tasks that would otherwise suck up really large computational resources, such as rendering graphics or video processing, are far more approachable and quicker.

2) Generative Models: Apple Intelligence implements sophisticated, generative models that give users new ways of creating and manipulating content. For example, AI-driven features in

creative applications may offer design suggestions or automatically enhance video edits.

ON-DEVICE PROCESSING TOGETHER WITH PRIVATE CLOUD COMPUTE

1) Enhanced Privacy Protection: Apple Intelligence is unique in its respect for user privacy. Operations are done on the device itself, keeping sensitive data local to reduce the threat from the outside world. In other words, this security makes sure personal information remains private while using much-desired AI functionality.

2) Private Cloud Compute for Complex Tasks: Apple Intelligence opens the way for Private Cloud Compute for tasks that require more computational power. Larger AI models housed in servers become accessible to the users, while retaining solid privacy features. Any data passed to the cloud enjoys the latest encryption and security processes so that the safety of users' personal data is guaranteed.

INNOVATIVE COMMUNICATION AND SELF-EXPRESSION TOOLS

1) Smart Communication Features: Apple Intelligence amplifies communication by allowing and enabling the features for more productive communication. This could be in the form of smart sorting of emails, intelligent response suggestions, or context-sensitive text proposals that speed up messaging and correspondence.

They allow users to pay more attention to their work without being burdened with routine tasks and hence boost overall productivity.

2) Creative Expression: Apple Intelligence runs the gamut from creative applications and can extend to actually helping users express themselves in the most constructive possible light. For example, AI could suggest creative content, format documents automatically, or enhance images with smart filters-all courtesy of the system's intelligence.

FUTURE-PROOFING THE MAC EXPERIENCE

1) Continuous Learning and Adaptation: With time, Apple Intelligence is engineered to learn and evolve with the user's interactions-accurately predicting and recommending items. In this respect, the more a user works on their iMac M4, the more the operating system becomes sensitive to how they work; hence, the experience grows more efficient and personalized with use.

2) Compatibility with macOS Sequoia: macOS Sequoia has integrated Apple Intelligence so that users enjoy the latest features and improvements regarding AI capabilities and the design of user interface interactions. It's facilitated with seamless updates for enhancements to keep users at the bleeding edge.

ENVIRONMENT FRIENDLY

The new iMac with the M4 begins to showcase Apple's commitment to the environment with innovative designs and sourcing of materials responsibly. This iMac, with a number of eco-friendly features, furthers the user experience and aligns with Apple's ambitious goals for environmental stewardship. An extended discussion of features that make the iMac M4 better for the environment is presented herein.

RECYCLED MATERIALS

1) Aluminum Blended from Recycled Sources: The new iMac stand features 100% recycled aluminum, which reduces the carbon footprint from mining and processing virgin aluminum. This program speaks to Apple's approach in reducing waste while enabling circular economy practices, meaning collecting materials for recycling to reuse rather than relying only upon new resources.

2) Recycled Gold, Tin, as well as Copper: Recycling gold plating and using a process like eutectic tin soldering of its components increases the sustainability factor in the production of the iMac. By making use of such elements manufactured from recyclable materials, Apple reduces demand for newly mined metals, that are often mined under very poor mining practices causing high environmental degradation. In addition, copper in printed circuit boards is also sourced from

recycled materials, as would be expected in an integrated approach towards sustainable design.

ENERGY EFFICIENCY STANDARDS

1) High Energy Efficiency: The iMac M4 also meets Apple's strict criteria for energy efficiency, which is an essential consideration in ensuring that it uses the minimum quantity of energy in operation. This helps not only in reducing costs of operation by the user but also reduces the impact on the environment consequent to generation of electricity, mainly using fossil fuels.

2) Eco-Friendly Design: Besides its energy consumption alone, the design of the iMac allows for efficient cooling and performance in ensuring that energy use is optimized for a wide array of tasks. This attention to efficiency, in turn, supports a more sustainable life cycle for products.

ELIMINATION OF HARMFUL MATERIALS

1) Mercury-Free Displays: The iMac is designed to be free of mercury, which is one of the deadliest toxins used in electronic components. Such commitment to toxic material elimination makes all the difference in terms of reducing the environmental footprint and assurance of product safety.

2) Brominated Flame Retardants and PVC-free: The absence of PVC and flame retardants containing bromine in the materials iMac uses also shows

that Apple has an interest in making less harmful but environmental-friendly products. These chemicals emit toxic gases into the ecosystem when their life cycles are being processed, and the exclusion results in a cleaner and safe ecosystem.

SUSTAINABLE PACKAGING
1) Fibre-Based Packaging: The new iMac packaging incorporates 100% fibre-based materials, a significant leap for Apple in its packaging. It enacts Apple's commitment to removing plastic materials in packaging by 2025, part of the measures that are necessary in cutting plastic waste that results in landfills and oceans.
2) Minimalist Packaging Design: The eco-friendly packaging not only serves a functional purpose but also is a reflection of a minimalist design approach that reduces the excess use of materials. This well-thought design supports furthering sustainability by minimizing waste in the packaging process.

CARBON NEUTRAL GOALS
1) Corporate Carbon Neutrality: Apple has reached carbon neutrality for all its global corporate operations, representing a serious commitment to carbon footprint reduction. The iMac M4 forms part of this wider reach where all products must fall under the positive light that Apple is trying to undergo environmentally.

2) Apple 2030 Goal: Apple leads the industry with its ambitious commitment to carbon neutrality across its entire supply chain and product life by 2030, which covers assessing and improving the energy efficiency in manufacturing processes using renewable energy. This also involves optimizing its logistics to reduce emissions.

WIDER ENVIRONMENTAL IMPACT
1) Promoting Sustainable Practices: By integrating these environment-friendly aspects into the iMac M4, Apple is setting an example and encouraging other companies in this industry to go greener. The company places much focus on recycled materials and energy efficiency to such an extent that it has set the benchmark for environmental responsibility within the circle of consumer electronics.
2) Consumer Awareness: Apple is pretty transparent regarding its environmental contributions, and this tends to help increase consumer awareness in respect of the role sustainability plays in technology. Thus, Apple manages to create an environmental care culture among its clients by using greener products, enticing them to reflect on the ecological implications of their purchases.

PRICING & AVAILABILITY

The new iMac M4 carries forward the mantle of Apple's tradition in terms of offering solution paths of different sizes while keeping the performance, design, and ecosystem integration at high levels both in pricing and availability. Allow me to dive deep into some features of the iMac M4 with regard to pricing, configuration methods, and customer support.

PRICING STRUCTURE

1) Entry-Level Model: Prices for the iMac M4 start from RM5,799 for the base model featuring an 8-core CPU, 8-core GPU, 16GB of unified memory (expandable to 24GB), and a 256GB SSD storage capacity that can be increased all the way to 1TB. For sure, this is a pretty good performance that will be more than enough for either a student, professional, or regular user.

2) Pricings for Education: Prices for the educational variants start from a rather reasonable RM5,579, which is more affordable for students and teachers. This is a pricing strategy to help penetrate more educational institutions with Apple products and enhance learning by experiencing powerful technology.

3) Enhanced Model: Prices for the iMac with 10-core CPU and GPU start from RM6,699, or RM6,269 with education discount. It comes with a massive 16GB unified memory, a value which is configurable up to 32GB, a 256GB SSD that could be configured up to 2TB, four Thunderbolt 4 ports, and an improved Magic Keyboard featuring Touch ID. The higher specs target those who require more power in processing; therefore, this

fits creative professionals and users with heavy applications of multitasking.

COLOR AND DESIGN VARIANTS
The new iMac is available in a range of vibrant colors such as green, pink, purple, bright yellow, orange, and blue, on top of silver. Users can, therefore, pick a model that shows their character or best fits the surroundings at work. The color options reveal Apple's commitment to individuality and inspiration, as manifested in the design style it has traditionally adopted for the iMac.

TECHNICAL SPECIFICATIONS
1) Unified Memory: This also leads to faster performance due to the iMac M4 unified memory architecture, where frequently used data can be pulled out much quicker and multitasking is allowed on a good efficiency rate. Choices go all the way up to 32GB, which will enable running applications that will take up plenty of memory with much ease, including graphic design, video editing, and software development.
2) Storage Options: These go up to 2TB from there, meaning one can choose how much storage fits based on large files, applications, and creative projects one may work on. The SSDs will ensure decent read/write speeds, translating into general system responsiveness.
3) Thunderbolt 4 Connectivity: Where the high variant is concerned, Thunderbolt 4 ports extend

connectivities in every direction with high data transfer rates and the ability to hook up multiple high-resolution displays, making it perfect for professionals who usually work with complex setups.

TRADE-IN PROGRAM

Apple's Trade In program lets customers turn in their old computer for up to credit for a new Mac. The program supports a customer's upgrade while helping Apple build on its commitment to the environment by making sure devices are recycled responsibly and repurposed. Customers can visit apple.com/my/shop/trade-in to see estimated device value and learn how to trade in their current Mac for credit toward an iMac purchase.

SOFTWARE AND FEATURE UPDATES

1) • Apple Intelligence: Apple Intelligence is a no-cost key software feature update that is coming to Macs with M1 and later processors. It will be supported by the new iMac M4, offering users more interaction thanks to generative models and on-device processing, while keeping privacy protections intact. It is launching in U.S. English, with support for more languages arriving over the next few months to further make the operating system inclusive for users around the world.

2) macOS Sequoia: The iMac comes loaded with macOS Sequoia 15.1, offering up iPhone mirroring, reimagined Safari to enrich browsing

tools, and much more in order to give one a fully immersive gaming experience. All this software will be integrated so that the users can improve their productivity and creativity on the new iMac.

APPLECARE+ FOR MAC

As such, AppleCare+ for Mac is unique in its kind of unprecedented service and support when it provides for:

1) Unlimited Incidents of Accidental Damage :This coverage gives the user confidence in case they damage their devices, for repairs can be done at a fixed service fee.
2) Battery Service Coverage: Users will have confidence in the fact that their Mac will remain usable for a longer period as they can have battery service coverage for their device.
3) 24/7 Support: Round-the-clock support by knowledgeable Apple professionals lets users seek help at any time, increasing the overall ownership experience.

CHAPTER 2: SETTING UP YOUR NEW IMAC

When setting up a new iMac, it is important to go through each setup option carefully in order for the configuration to be just right. The setup process in and of itself is not overly complicated; however, it does take some time-particularly if you plan on reviewing and adjusting each available setting.

These steps are good for any new Mac whether that's an iMac or a MacBook. Note that for this tutorial, we assume you have a brand new iMac and are setting it up from scratch.

To start working on a new Mac, you will want to set this up with the appropriate settings so that it's ready to use. Generally, setup is quite easy and doesn't take much time; however, it can if you want to go through each setting to turn some options on and off or change them.

SET LOCATION AND ACCESSIBILITY SETTINGS

After you power up your iMac, select your country or region. You can then turn on the features in accessibility to help you if you have problems with eyesight, hearing, and other items. If you want to set any of these, tap accordingly. Otherwise, you may tap "Not Now" to continue and later set them in case you may require them.

CONNECT TO WI-FI

Next, your iMac will connect you to a Wi-Fi network. Select the network you want, enter the password, and tap Continue. You will then proceed to a page highlighting the privacy policy regarding your data. Tap the link Learn More if you want more; otherwise, tap Continue and proceed.

TRANSFER DATA WITH MIGRATION ASSISTANT

You will now be given the opportunity to use Migration Assistant-a utility that transfers data from another Mac, a Time Machine backup, or a Windows PC. If you have any content to migrate, you can select the correct option and follow the on-screen instructions to complete the transfer. If you want to skip this step, tap "Not Now." You can still use Migration Assistant to transfer data later-even after you've completely set up your iMac.

Migration Assistant

If you have information on another Mac or a Windows PC, you can transfer it to this Mac. You can also transfer information from a Time Machine backup or another startup disk.

How do you want to transfer your information?

○ From a Mac, Time Machine backup or Startup disk
From a Windows PC

Not Now   Back   Continue

SET UP APPLE ID AND LOGIN

Sign in next with your Apple ID or create a new one if you don't have an account yet. An Apple ID is required to access most of the Apple services. If two-factor authentication is enabled for the Apple ID, enter the verification code sent to the iPhone or iPad.

Click Continue and then review the terms and conditions for iCloud.

Sign In with Your Apple ID

Sign in to use iCloud, the App Store, and other Apple services.

Apple ID

Create new Apple ID...

Forgot Apple ID or password?

Use different Apple IDs for iCloud and Apple media purchases?

This Mac will be associated with your Apple ID and data such as photos, contacts, and documents will be stored in iCloud so you can access them on other devices. See how your data is managed...

Set Up Later   Back   Continue

CREATE A COMPUTER ACCOUNT

At the Computer Account screen, first confirm your full name and create an account name that you will be using to login into your Mac. Then, Type your password for the account and a password hint if you want so you might not forget it later. Put the check alongside "Allow my Apple ID to reset this password" to make account recovery easier should you forget your password.

To personalize your account even further, tap the image alongside your account name to choose a Memoji, emoji, monogram, or photo. Tap Continue once you have customized your account to your satisfaction.

Create a Computer Account

Fill out the following information to create your computer account.

Full name: Lance Whitney

Account name: lancewhitney
This will be the name of your home folder.

Password: ●●●●●●●●●●●●●●●● ●●●●●●●●●●●●●●●●

Hint:

☑ Allow my Apple ID to reset this password

Back   Continue

KNOW THE FIND MY APP

The next screen provides you with some information about the Find My app. This is helpful because it serves to let you locate your Mac if it becomes lost. Taking a minute to understand how this works can also give you peace of mind, knowing that should this ever happen to you, you have ways of tracking your device.

MAKE THIS YOUR NEW MAC

You will be taken to the "Make This Your New Mac" screen where you can go through and change a number of different settings. You may click Continue to take all defaults for all the settings or at the bottom, you can click Customize Settings to change some options for Location Services, Analytics, and Siri.

59

Under Location Services, you are able to enable/disable location-based apps: Apple Maps and Weather.

You also have to select your time zone: you can either choose it from the drop-down list or click on a place in the map.

Select Your Time Zone

To select a time zone, click the map near your location and choose a city from the Closest City menu.
You can also have the time zone change automatically, if possible, based on your current location.

Set time zone automatically using current location

Time Zone: Eastern Standard Time
Closest City: New York, NY - United States

Back   Continue

Next, you want to decide if you will share analytics data with Apple. If you want further information on how data are collected and used, click the About Analytics and Privacy link.

Finally, if you'd like to be able to limit which apps and which websites have access to your iMac, you might want to enable **Screen Time**. To configure this later you can click **Set Up Later**.

Screen Time

Get insights about your screen time and set limits for what you want to manage.

Weekly Reports
View daily and weekly charts and get insights about your screen time.

Downtime and App Limits
Schedule time away from the screen and set daily time limits for apps or app categories.

Content & Privacy Restrictions
Restrict settings for contacts, explicit content, purchases and downloads, and privacy.

Screen Time Passcode
Manage screen time for children from your Mac or iOS device, or use a screen time passcode on your child's device.

Set Up Later   Back   Continue

ENABLE AND CONFIGURE SIRI

61

In the opened window, check the box labeled Enable Siri. This will turn on Apple's voice assistant for your iMac and provide a hands-free way to interact with your computer. Once you flip that switch to enable Siri, you're taken through a series of screens where you're asked to say certain phrases, because Siri wants to get a little more familiar with your voice.

Siri

Siri helps you get things done just by asking. Siri can also make suggestions before you ask in apps, search, and keyboards.

☑ Enable Ask Siri

Apple stores transcripts of your interactions with Siri and may review a subset of these transcripts. Siri may also send information like your voice input, Hey Siri setup, contacts, and location to Apple to process your request. Data is not associated with your Apple ID.
About Ask Siri, Dictation & Privacy...

Back   Continue

If it doesn't bother you that Apple will have access to your recordings to help improve Siri, check the box next to **Share Audio Recordings**. The data enables Apple's voice recognition to fine tune its service and also aids in improving Siri in general. Tap the About Improve Siri and Dictation & Privacy link for additional details about how your recorded audio is used and stored.

Improve Siri & Dictation

Help Apple improve Siri and Dictation by allowing Apple to store audio of your Siri and Dictation interactions from this Mac. Apple may review a sample of stored audio. You can change this later in System Preferences.

This data is not associated with your Apple ID, and will only be stored for a limited period.

Share Audio Recordings
○ Not Now

About Improve Siri and Dictation & Privacy...

Back   Continue

Of course, if you don't want to do that, then select Not Now. That way you keep all of your audio recordings private, though you'll still be able to use Siri for basic functions. Of course you can always go back into Settings later and turn this on.

SET UP FILEVAULT FOR DISK ENCRYPTION

Once Siri is set up, you will be asked whether you want to turn on FileVault disk encryption on your iMac. FileVault is a security option that encrypts your entire disk so data is kept safe and resistant to unauthorized access. To turn this extra layer of security on, select **Turn on FileVault disk encryption**.

FileVault Disk Encryption

FileVault secures your data by encrypting the contents of your disk and locking your screen with a password.

Would you like to use FileVault to encrypt the disk on your Mac?

☑ Turn on FileVault disk encryption
☑ Allow my iCloud account to unlock my disk

Your iCloud account "lance@lancewhit.com" can be used to unlock your disk and reset your password if you forget it. If you do not want to allow your iCloud account to reset your password, you can create a recovery key and store it in a safe place to unlock your disk.

Back   Continue

You can further enhance your security by selecting the box beside Allow my iCloud account to unlock my disk. If you can't recall your password on Mac, you may be relieved to know this method will afford you another way to access your encrypted disk without manually going through some kind of reset process.

SET UP TOUCH ID (IF AVAILABLE)

If your iMac includes Touch ID, you should set that up next. Click **Continue** and follow the onscreen prompts to enroll your fingerprint. You will have to place and remove your finger a couple of times onto the power button until your fingerprint is registered. That way, Touch ID will be able to recognize your finger for its safe unlocking later. When Touch ID is ready, click **Continue**.

CHOOSE A DESKTOP THEME

Next, you'll have the option to choose a theme for your desktop after setting up Touch ID: Light Mode,

Dark Mode, or Auto. Light Mode is bright and shiny, while Dark Mode is sleek and much easier on the eyes in low-lit environments. The Auto option will change the themes according to your time of day, seamlessly transitioning between light and dark mode.

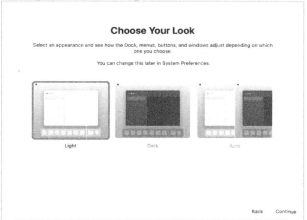

Even after the default setting when you first set up your system, later in life, you can change how you prefer your theme through the Display settings. This will give you flexibility in order to personalize your visual experience due to personal preference or certain lighting conditions.

UPDATE YOUR MAC

Once this is done, you'll be whisked away to the desktop of your newly set-up iMac. The final important thing you'll want to do is update your Mac-you want the most recent version of macOS for many reasons, one of which is new features. Also, critical patches and bug fixes are added.

The first thing to do to update is to open the System Settings: Click the Apple menu located at the top left of your screen. Next, click General, followed by Software Update. It will check under this section for any updates. If there were any available updates, it may ask for your password for your Mac. Just insert the password and click Update or Install, and it will let it download and install itself.

Those using Macs with macOS Monterey or an operating system earlier than this will have the steps slightly different. Click the Apple icon located in the top left, and then click About This Mac. Under this menu choice, select Software Update; you will be taken to the update screen as described above. You will see if there is an update available. Click Upgrade Now to start installing.

This may take some time after having launched the update process, as your Mac needs to download the files to do so. The length of time depends on the update size and your Internet connection. Once the files have finished downloading, installation will begin.

During this, your Mac will restart a few times. When it finally comes to a stop after the last reboot, it returns you to the login page from whence you will have to log in with your credentials. You'll log into a now-updated iMac with the latest software enhancements that guarantee a much easier and more secure usage experience.

Watching for updates will keep your Mac current and support all the improvements Apple makes to the OS. This last step will ensure not only that your new iMac is fully prepared to run at optimal levels but that you too are prepared with new, updated features and safety enhancements.

CHAPTER 3: USING ICLOUD WITH YOUR IMAC

iCloud allows your iMac to interact seamlessly with other devices from Apple, keeping information such as documents, photos, and other data from your iPhone, iPad, or even Apple Watch in sync. Using the same Apple ID on all of them, iCloud will make sure you get any document, photo, and anything else at any given time so that you're always up to date and collaborate with your family and friends in the smoothest manner.

SIGNING IN AND SETTING UP ICLOUD

If you didn't enable iCloud during the initial setup of your iMac, you can still activate it anytime by following these steps:

1. Open System Settings: From your iMac desktop, click on the Apple menu in the upper-left corner of the screen and choose System Settings.
2. Sign in with Apple Account: The System Settings sidebar will have the option saying Sign in with your Apple Account. Click on it and log in with your Apple ID and password if you haven't already.
3. Turn on iCloud: After logging in, you will have an iCloud option. Click on that and toggle on the features according to preference.

CONFIGURING ICLOUD FEATURES

Some of the aspects in iCloud are immensely helpful, and you can opt to enable them or turn them off, depending on your needs. The following include:

1. iCloud Drive: You can enable iCloud Drive to store documents securely, and they will appear on all your devices. Also, any edit you do to a file on one of them instantly updates across all your other devices connected by your Apple ID.

2. Photos: These you will share with the iCloud Photos feature, enabling you to update photos and videos on either your iPhone, iPad, or iMac and then view them on any other device linked with the same account. • Mail, Contacts, and Calendar: Keep your mail, contacts, and calendar events up to date across your devices. It's quite helpful if you really rely on e-mail, your contact list, and your calendar or reminders.

3. Messages iCloud: This is an option used to keep your messages updated across devices, so that conversations appear uniformly regardless of whether you are working in your iMac, iPhone, or iPad.

4. Safari: In regards to Safari, turn on iCloud and all of your bookmarks, tabs, and browsing history will be in sync between your devices, serving to facilitate an easy switch between your various devices.

5. Find My Mac: This iCloud security feature enables you to locate your iMac if it ever gets stolen or lost. You are given the opportunity to remotely lock or erase your device if it is necessary.

The items above are toggled on or off in the settings for iCloud. These give you options on which items you want to sync and access across multiple devices.

iCloud does not only allow you to sync across different devices but enables sharing where one can share folders, documents-even albums-with others. You might want to do this for working on projects with colleagues, organizing family photos, or sharing files with friends.

USING YOUR IMAC WITH OTHER DEVICES

With Continuity, you can do the following with your iMac and other Apple devices that are signed in with the same Apple ID and connected to the same Wi-Fi network. Continuity provides several useful-and creative-ways to move what you're doing from one gadget to another:

1. Handoff: You can begin using one gadget and continue what where you stopped on another. Examples: You can start an email or a document on the iPhone and then finish it on the iMac using Handoff. To pick up on another device, simply click the Handoff icon in your iMac's Dock or your iPhone/iPad app switcher.
2. iPhone as Webcam: Your iMac comes with Continuity Camera, that enables the use of your iPhone as a high-quality webcam. To use it, initiate a video call from any application, such as FaceTime, from your iMac while keeping the

iPhone in its proximity. The iMac will instantly identify and pair with your iPhone's camera to bring you the benefits of higher resolution, along with Portrait mode and Centre Stage.

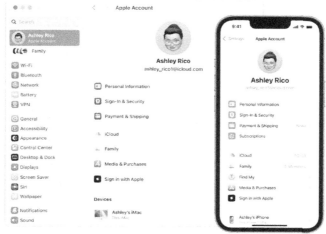

3. AirPlay: AirPlay enables streaming of what is on your iMac to another compatible Apple device: such as a Mac, iPhone, and Apple TV. Great for either giving presentations, showing someone photos, or just watching videos on a bigger screen. You open the AirPlay menu on your iMac and select which device you want to stream to.

4. Sidecar: This is going to let the use of your iPad as extended display for your iMac. That's great for having extended workspace or multitasking without necessarily having another monitor. With the feature called Sidecar, go through your settings in the iMac and under Display settings, you will get a suggestion to add your nearby iPad as an extra display.

5. Universal Clipboard: Copy on one device, paste on another. For example, you copy some text or an image on your iMac and directly paste it into a note or email on your iPhone or iPad, streamlining the workflow between all your devices.

ACCESSING ICLOUD CONTENT ON YOUR IMAC

First set up iCloud on your iMac, and have instant access to, and sync key content such as photos, files, notes, and passwords across all your Apple devices. Here's a close look at how iCloud keeps data connected and accessible on your iMac and beyond.

SETTING UP ICLOUD ON YOUR IMAC

1. Make Sure iCloud Is Turned On: If you didn't turn on iCloud during the setup process, open System Settings and click Apple ID; after that, sign in with your Apple ID. Further, select iCloud to turn it on.
2. Select iCloud Features: This will bring you to the options of all various things that are available to be selected, such as Photos, iCloud Drive, Notes, Safari, and Keychain. Turn on each feature you'd like to sync with iCloud; this information stores itself in the cloud and allows syncing automatically across your Apple devices.
3. Manage Your Storage: Apple provides everyone with 5 GB of free iCloud storage, but you can upgrade to iCloud+ to get more storage and other

premium features. To check or upgrade your storage, go to System Settings > Apple ID > iCloud > Manage Storage. The iCloud+ plans house up to 2TB of storage alongside advanced features such as Private Relay and Hide My Email that help in privacy.

ACCESSING YOUR ICLOUD CONTENT

After setting up iCloud on your iMac, you'll have easy access to your content through several apps and locations that are specifically dedicated:

1. Photos: All the photos taken and videos recorded from your iPhone, iPad, or other Apple device will automatically appear in the Photos app on your iMac. Open the Photos app to view, organize, and edit your images. Edits made on one device will be synced to all other devices, though you can elect to store full-resolution images on iCloud and lighter-resolution versions on your devices to save space.

2. iCloud Drive: You can access iCloud Drive directly from Finder on your iMac for an easy way to save and manage files and folders in the cloud. You can drag files into iCloud Drive to access them from any other device signed into your Apple ID. For instance, a document saved to iCloud Drive on your iMac can be opened and edited on your iPhone or iPad.

3. Notes: If you have Notes set to sync with iCloud, then your notes will stay up-to-date across all your devices. You write a note on your iMac, and voil`,

it's there in an instant on your iPhone, iPad, or other Apple devices.

4. Reminders and Calendars: Set up to-dos and appointments using Reminders and the Calendar app. You can have everything automatically set up across all your devices. Anything you edit or create on one device instantly updates everywhere.

5. iCloud Keychain: iCloud Keychain lets you save and share passwords, credit card numbers, and even Wi-Fi networks securely across the devices. It makes sure you always have the credentials you need for login on any device while keeping all this information encrypted for extra security. Keychain is controlled in System Settings > Passwords in your iMac.

6. Safari Bookmarks and Tabs: These are also across devices with the use of Safari; just like your bookmarks, browsing history, and open tabs automatically keep themselves in sync. With Handoff or directly opening up open tabs through Safari, you can open a web page on your iOS device and pick up right where you stopped on your iMac.

ICLOUD+ BENEFITS

iCloud+ is an optional, paid upgrade to iCloud that affords you additional tools which could actually help with storage, privacy, and even collaboration. Here's what iCloud+ can do for you:

1. Expanded Storage: iCloud+ allows you to expand your storage beyond iCloud's free 5GB allowance.

74

Plans start at 50GB and go up to 2TB, providing plenty of space for files, photos, backups, and more. You can share your iCloud+ storage plan with as many as five family members using Family Sharing.

2. Private Relay in iCloud: Private Relay refers to one of those privacy features related to encrypting your internet traffic during activity in Safari, hiding IP addresses to protect identity. It sends your internet activity through multiple servers, making it much harder for websites to track the online action.

3. HomeKit Secure Video: Recordings from smart security cameras can be stored securely by HomeKit with iCloud+, which doesn't take away your iCloud storage. This service includes end-to-end encryption, which means only you and the person you give access to will be able to see the recordings.

4. Custom Email Domain: This feature helps you connect your custom email domain to your iCloud account for sending and receiving emails with a personalized domain, such as "yourname@yourdomain.com." It makes communications sound more professional while still being hooked up with iCloud Mail.

SYNCING ACROSS ALL DEVICES

Once you set up iCloud on your iMac and all your other devices, Apple's ecosystem works in concert to automatically keep everything in sync. Use the same

Apple ID on all of them, and voil-versa: files, photos, passwords, etc., appear everywhere. This further allows fluid and practically painless device switching, as iCloud works to put whatever you need at your fingertips-be it on your iMac, iPhone, iPad, or Apple Watch.

AUTOMATICALLY SAVE YOUR DESKTOP AND DOCUMENTS TO ICLOUD DRIVE WITH YOUR IMAC

Set up iCloud Drive to automatically save both your Desktop and Documents folders, and access your most-used files easier on all of your Apple devices. In such a case, any document that you would have saved on the Desktop or in the Documents folder of your iMac will immediately show up in the iCloud Drive, hence making it easy for you to access and update them from any other device of your choice. Here's how it works, and how to set it up:

1. HOW ICLOUD DRIVE WORKS WITH DESKTOP AND DOCUMENTS

By placing files on the Desktop or in the Documents folder on iCloud Drive, you create one spot for frequently accessed files. When you have iCloud Drive set up for the Desktop and Documents of a device:

1. The files that are stored in those folders are transferred to iCloud Drive and then immediately synced to other Apple devices that have the same Apple ID signed in to them.
2. You can access your files from anywhere—your iPhone, iPad, or another Mac—and even on non-Apple devices at iCloud.com or with the iCloud for Windows app.
3. Changes you make to files in these folders will be updated in real time across all your devices, so you're always working with the most current version.

This setup is ideal for working with document, spreadsheet, and image files that you're always updating, so that it's easy to switch between devices.

2. HOW TO CONFIGURE ICLOUD DRIVE FOR DESKTOP AND DOCUMENTS ON YOUR IMAC

To configure, follow these steps:

1. Launch System Settings: On your iMac screen, from the top left, click the Apple menu and then select System Settings.
2. Click on Apple Account: On the sidebar, click on your Apple Account.

3. Enable iCloud Drive: Go to menu, select iCloud, then click on iCloud Drive.
4. Select Desktop and Documents Folders: You will notice you can choose the option to enable syncing for Desktop and Documents folders. This will save those particular folders in iCloud Drive. Confirm your selection in order to proceed.

3. ACCESSING YOUR FILES ACROSS DEVICES

Once you have enabled iCloud Drive for Desktop and Documents:
1. iPhone/iPad: After opening the Files app and going to iCloud Drive, you will notice that there are two folders: Desktop and Documents. Anything you save to those folders on your iMac will appear here.
2. iCloud.com: For any web browser use your Apple ID to access your iCloud account at iCloud.com. Proceed to click on the iCloud Drive icon to access your files remotely.
3. From a Windows PC: From a Windows PC, begin by downloading & installing iCloud for Windows. Subsequently, you will have access to the files stored in your iCloud Drive. Files on the iMac that are stored in the Desktop and Documents folders can also appear in the iCloud Drive section on Windows.

4. BENEFITS OF STORING FILES WITHIN ICLOUD DRIVE

By having Desktop and Documents in iCloud Drive, you are able to:

1. Cloud Work: Your files are available on any device that has access to the internet. You can start working on a document on your iMac and then pick up right where you stopped from your iPhone, or even your iPad.
2. Automatic Backups: The files in iCloud Drive will also create a backup in iCloud. It forms an extra layer of security. If your iMac is lost, stolen, or suffers some kind of hardware failure, your files are safe in iCloud.
3. Partitioning Space: It automatically manages the storage of your iMac by moving the older files to iCloud. The files are still accessible; however, because of inactive use, they remain stored in iCloud, which frees the local storage.

5. APPLY CHANGES AND DEVICE SYNCHRONIZATION

Any change or modification you make in the file on your iMac will be saved automatically to iCloud Drive and will be reflected instantly on another device.

1. Open and Edit Files: When you open a file on your iMac, it downloads locally for immediate editing. When you save, it syncs back with iCloud Drive so any other connected devices have the latest version.

2. Offline Access: When opening files on your iMac, they store locally so they will be accessible offline. If changes were made offline, they will sync back up with iCloud Drive when reconnected to the internet.

6. MANAGE STORAGE AND ICLOUD+

Each Apple ID is provided with 5 GB of free storage on iCloud, but iCloud+ provides the option to get more capacity along with additional premium features. You could upgrade to iCloud+ if you intend to keep a substantial amount of files or even larger types of files like videos or high-resolution images.

7. MORE ON USING ICLOUD DRIVE

1. Organize Files: Utilize folders in iCloud Drive to ensure a manageable Desktop and Documents across devices.
2. Manage Your iMac Storage: With System Settings opening > select Apple ID > tap iCloud Drive, then toggle the button next to Optimize Mac Storage. This method will save space by storing only recently accessed files on your iMac while keeping others available in iCloud.
3. Sync Only What You Need: If you feel that iCloud Drive is syncing way too much data, then you can enable Desktop and Documents syncing to have certain files only on your iMac.

CHAPTER 4: STORING AND SHARING PHOTOS WITH ICLOUD ON YOUR IMAC

iCloud Photos allows you to access your entire photo and video collection, or share any amount of them, with ease across all your devices. Once iCloud Shared Photo Library is turned on, a space for shared media will be opened with other individuals, where each person can add photos, make edits, and even comment in real time. Here's how to set up both features and maximize their full potential.

1. SETTING UP ICLOUD PHOTOS ON YOUR IMAC

iCloud Photos keeps all your photos and videos in sync across your iMac, iPhone, iPad, and other Apple devices connected with the same Apple ID. Whatever edits, deletions, or additions you make on one device will reflect on all your other devices.

1. Turn On System Settings: Open Your iMac's System Settings.
2. iCloud Sign in: Go to your Apple Account inside the sidebar and click iCloud.
3. Turn On iCloud Photos: Under the iCloud settings, locate Photos, then turn it on. That'll cause iCloud to start syncing your photos and videos.

Once you have iCloud Photos turned on, it automatically launches the upload of your iMac's

Photos library media files to iCloud. You can then proceed to view or manage your photos from any device through its Photos app or via iCloud.com using non-Apple devices.

2. BENEFITS OF STORING YOUR PHOTOS IN ICLOUD PHOTOS

By enabling iCloud Photos on iMac, it does the following:
1. Keeps Your Library Up-to-Date: It keeps all of your media and its edits up to date across each connected device. You will always have the most recent photo or video versions with you.
2. Provides a Safe Storage: iCloud gives safe backup for your photos and videos. If some problems appear with your iMac, you will have the media in iCloud.
3. Optimizes Storage: macOS turns on the Optimize Mac Storage option by default in order to save storage. With this, iCloud contains full-resolution photos and videos, while your iMac contains optimized versions to ensure at least local storage usage.

3. SETTING UP AND MANAGING ICLOUD SHARED PHOTO LIBRARY

With iCloud Photos, you can share a photo library with as many as five people. That's how you get to share memories and moments with them. This will make all the members entitled to add, edit, and comment on the photos and videos so that it becomes shared space for each.

1. Open Photos: Open the Photos app on your iMac.
2. Access Shared Library Settings: In the Photos app, go to Photos > Settings in the menu bar and then select the Shared Library tab.
3. Follow Onscreen Instructions: Tap Get Started to set up your Shared Library; follow the on-screen prompts that will pop up, inviting up to five others.

INVITING PEOPLE AND SHARING PHOTOS

You can add members in it by inviting them through Messages or Email. After accepting the invitation, they have access and are able to add items to the shared library.

Adding Content to the Shared Library:
You are able to explicitly choose what photos and videos you'd like to share or use Smart Suggestions to add media based on your criteria such as:

1. Photos of specific people, using face detection,
2. Photos taken at specific places,
3. Pictures taken on a specific date or during some event.

This saves time and helps ensure that such important memories are not only located easily but also shared with people who matter.

4. HOW TO USE ICLOUD SHARED PHOTO LIBRARY FEATURES

In front of a Shared Library, everyone has equal rights to add or remove photos and videos, make edits, and add comments, which is highly collaborative. Unique features include:

1. Real-time Updates: Whatever one person edits gets updated in real time for everyone.
2. Edits and Comments: One can edit photos, including the usual ones like brightness and cropping, and even add comments for a collaborative feel.
3. Smart Curation: The AI in iCloud goes one step further to suggest the adding of photos, such as those with specific people or taken on specific dates.

5. MANAGING ICLOUD STORAGE

iCloud Storage provides 5 GB of storage with every Apple ID, and that fills up pretty fast if photos and videos are involved. To take on a larger library or add Shared Library members, you can: ICO

1. Upgrade to iCloud+: iCloud+ plans give extra storage and add premium features, which may be key in your case to store a serious amount of photos and video.
2. iCloud+: It is allowed to share an iCloud+ plan with family members to share storage space without each person purchasing one.

6. VIEWING PHOTOS ON ALL DEVICES

Once iCloud Photos has been activated:
1. With iPhone/iPad: Launch the Photos application and view your entire library.
2. Using a Windows PC: Set up iCloud for Windows; access your photos from File Explorer.
3. On iCloud.com: Sign in to iCloud.com using your Apple ID, then click on iCloud Photos.

7. PRIVACY AND SECURITY WITH ICLOUD PHOTOS

Apple puts a lot of importance on user privacy and especially when dealing with iCloud Photos. The feature is encrypted on an end-to-end basis; hence, only you and those whom you share the data with will access your photos and videos. Data encrypted in iCloud is stored by Apple, but Apple can never decrypt hence that data will remain private and secure.

ACCESS PURCHASES ANYWHERE WITH ICLOUD ON IMAC AND ENJOY

With iCloud, when you sign in to every one of your Apple devices using the same ID, it automatically syncs your purchases across your devices. Purchases through App Store, Apple TV app, Apple Books, and iTunes Store will show on all compatible devices that you sign in with your Apple ID. In particular, this is quite convenient for listening to music, watching movies, reading books, and using applications with your iMac, iPhone, and iPad, Apple TV, and even Windows computers with iTunes.

HOW TO ACCESS PURCHASES ON ALL DEVICES

1) Sign in using Apple ID: First, ensure you sign in to iCloud using one Apple ID for all devices; for your iMac: open System Settings, then click your Apple Account in the sidebar, and under Apple ID, confirm that you're signed in.
2) To View Purchases:
   a) Music: Open Apple Music on your iMac where you can view your purchased tracks, albums, and playlists.
   b) Apple TV App: The Apple TV app can be opened to view any movies or shows that have been purchased or rented.
   c) Books: With the Apple Books app, it's a snap to read any purchased eBooks or listen to any audiobooks.
   d) Apps: Any apps you have bought on one device also appear on other devices under the Purchased section in the App Store.

With iCloud, you can start watching a movie on Apple TV, continue on your iMac, and then continue from where you stopped on an iPad. iCloud keeps all of your purchases in the cloud.

BENEFITS OF PURCHASING WITH ICLOUD SYNCING

1) Convenience-iCloud keeps purchases in sync for easy access to media across devices without needing to download the same files on multiple devices.
2) Consistent Experience: With Apple devices, you can continue right from where you stopped while using a book, movie, song, and others, on another device.
3) Storage Optimization: iCloud+ allows you to store your purchase in the cloud; hence, saving your device storage by only downloading the stuff whenever the need arises.

USING FIND MY MAC TO PROTECT AND LOCATE YOUR IMAC

With Find My Mac, you can locate, lock, or even wipe your iMac from iCloud if it happens to be lost or stolen. If Find My Mac is enabled, then use the Find My app on other Apple devices or iCloud.com to locate the last known location of your iMac. It would have brought in peace of mind by availing options of remote access, which protect data in case your Mac is misplaced or compromised.

SETTING UP FIND MY MAC

1) Turn on the Find My Mac Feature
   a) Open System Settings in your iMac.

b) Click on the Apple Account from the sidebar. Now tap **iCloud**.
c) Under the iCloud settings, click Show All and toggle the **Find my Mac** to "on."
2) Using Find My Mac:
a) Locate Your Device: If your iMac was stolen, launch the Find My app on another device or go to iCloud.com, if you are on any other web browser. You could see it on a map here.
b) Lock the Screen: Remotely locking your iMac is possible. If you want to keep people from getting into your computer, and you can display a customized message when the screen is locked-on stuff like contact information.
c) Erase Data: If all else fails, then you can erase all data on your iMac for preventing access to any personal or sensitive data.

FIND MY MAC BENEFITS

1) Enhanced Security: Suppose someone tries to access your iMac; you can easily lock it from a distance to keep your data protected.
2) Mind Find My Mac provides you with the reassurance of knowing that although your iMac may be out of sight, you can take necessary steps in securing or recovering the same.
3) Remote Erase Knowing that you'll be able to erase all your data on Mac instantly in cases of an emergency adds to the security level, primarily concerning business or personal information.

ICLOUD'S ROLE IN UNIFYING YOUR APPLE EXPERIENCE

iCloud allows your purchases and devices to connect seamlessly with one another into one continuous ecosystem that's easily accessible anywhere. With Find My Mac, you secure access to your iMac without harming its safety. Both features, together, bring out the versatility and reliability of iCloud in simplifying your digital life while allowing you ways to protect it.

CHAPTER 5: NAVIGATING THE MAC OS INTERFACE

UNDERSTANDING THE LAYOUT: THE DESKTOP AND THE MENU BAR

When you first power up your iMac, you are greeted with the desktop. The desktop is the central workspace where you will spend most of your time working. Along the top is the menu bar, which houses all of the system functionality and application menus. Along the bottom you'll find the Dock, where you can access quick ways to get into your most-used applications and documents.

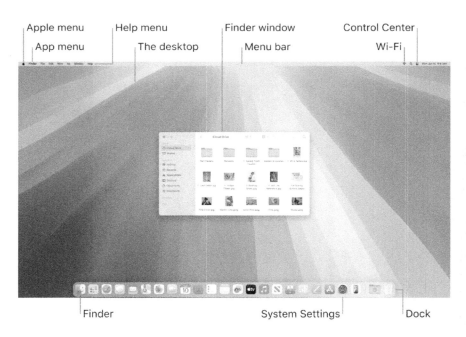

Apple menu   Help menu   Finder window   Control Center

App menu   The desktop   Menu bar   Wi-Fi

Finder   System Settings   Dock

Hint: If you are having trouble finding where your cursor is on the screen it can be temporarily magnified by quickly moving your finger back and forth on the trackpad. If using a mouse, try sliding it back and forth quickly.

DESKTOP FUNCTIONALITY

The desktop is the home base for your work. It's where you can open and work in applications, work with your files, and use Spotlight to search your iMac or the web. You can customize your desktop by changing your wallpaper. To do this, open System Settings, click Wallpaper inside the sidebar, and then select how you want to go about it.

You can also store files right on the desktop if that is how you roll. If you want your desktop to remain somewhat organized, you can use the stacks option, which lets you group similar files together, keeping clutter at bay.

THE MENU BAR

Along the top of your screen is the menu bar; this is a key element of macOS. It is the control room through which one can access other functions to carry out certain tasks inside applications. On the left-hand side, menus are context sensitive: the items that appear will change depending on what application you happen to have open at any one time. This adaptability allows for an efficient workflow in which commands and tools relevant to the opened application can be easily accessed by the user.

On the menu bar's right, there is a series of icons offering quick ways to access some of the important features. These include the following :

1) Wi-Fi Status: The Wi-Fi icon 📶 in the menu bar allows you to join a network or display information about your current connection.

2) Control Center: This icon 🎛 gives access to settings like brightness, volume, and Do Not Disturb.

3) Battery Charge: This icon 🔋 allows Mac users to easily see how much battery life they have remaining and opens up options to control your power settings.

4) Spotlight Search: The magnifying glass icon 🔍 is an easy way to search your Mac and the web to find whatever documents, applications, or anything you may need in an instant.

Using these menu items listed in the menu bar, you will be able to handle your tasks with ease and keep your productivity in good condition.

THE APPLE MENU

The Apple menu is important to the macOS experience and is found on the left-hand side of the screen. You can always open the Apple menu by clicking the Apple icon. It's where you'll find many of the frequently used items that create an easy-to-access link to several key functions.

In the Apple menu , you will be able to select:

1) About This Mac: See information about your Mac, including the model and which version of macOS you're using.
2) System Preferences: This opens the system preferences with which you can make changes to features and functionalities on your Mac.
3) Recent Items: This opens a list of all applications and documents that you have opened lately and offers quick access to the documents you have been working with.
4) Shut Down, Restart or Sleep: Just put your computer to sleep or restart/shut it down from here.

The Apple menu allows you to access some important system functionalities, adding convenience for you when you navigate through macOS.

APP MENU

One of the powerful features of macOS is the ability to run multiple applications and windows simultaneously. At any given time, the name of the active application is boldly type-faced to the right of

the Apple menu in the menu bar. To the right of the app name you will find its unique menus, which provide access to the functions and commands specific to that application.

If you switch to another application or click on an open window of another app, the name in the app menu changes. That means the menu options within the menu bar will change with the commands relevant to the newly active app. This dynamic updating ensures you continuously have access to the relevant tool set you need for your current task.

If you have opened a menu looking for a certain command and do not find it, remember to check whether the application in which you want to execute the command is the active application. If it is not, just click in the desired application window to bring it to the front, and the application menu bar will change to reflect the appropriate application commands .

THE HELP MENU

macOS provides great help options via the Help menu, which is always available via the menu bar. Using this feature, you can find your way around your iMac at any moment. In opening the help, in opening the Finder by clicking on it from the Dock. While in this environment, click on the Help menu and select macOS Help to open the macOS User Guide. The user guide is quite comprehensive and gives one a chance to go through troubleshooting and locating most of the operating system's features.

Alternatively, from any page in the Help menu, you can simply type your search term into the search box and click Return. As you start to type, suggestions will begin to show, making it easier to find what you want.

To use application-specific help, open an application, then from the menu bar click Help. This will give you context sensitive help so you can search for application-specific solutions related to the work you are trying to complete.

Tip: Maximize your desktop by making use of the widgets in your widget gallery. You can even share widgets with your desktop directly from your iPhone, and without having to download the corresponding app, the information needed will seamlessly appear at your fingertips.

CHAPTER 6: THE FINDER

Finder is one of the most important parts of macOS.

It is represented by a blue icon with a smiling face , and it's where you do the bulk of organizing and finding almost anything on your Mac, including documents, images, movies, and many other types of files. With Finder, you can manage your files and folders efficiently to continue with smooth workflow.

OPENING A FINDER WINDOW

Click the Finder icon, which appears in the Dock at the bottom of your screen. The Finder window opens, displaying a sidebar that provides easy access to your key locations, including Documents, Downloads, and Pictures. In this layout, you will find a way of navigating around your files.

QUICK VIEW AND EDITING FILES

Another of the more useful features of the Finder is that file icons respond to the Force Click function. By pressing firmly on a file icon, you pop open a quick view of its contents with it opening the file fully. That comes in pretty useful for identifying what might be inside a document or image. Also, if you want to edit the name of a file, by Force Clicking on the filename it becomes editable so that you can rename the file faster.

ORGANIZING

Your Mac has already created default folders for commonly used types of content: Documents, Pictures, Applications and Music. By default, these folders will automatically categorize your files. As you progress through writing documents, installing apps, or doing other work you may want to create additional folders for further organization.

To create a new folder, starting from the top of the screen, go into the Finder menu option File > New Folder. This action will create a new folder in the current location you are looking at and name it appropriately for related files with which you will store them. This organizational strategy helps maintain a clutter-free workspace and makes it easier to find your files when needed.

SYNCING DEVICES

When you connect a device to your Mac-say, an iPhone or an iPad-it becomes available right inside of

Finder. When attached, the integration of such a device becomes effortless: the name will automatically appear in the Finder sidebar.

All you have to do is click on the name of the device in your sidebar to manage your device. An interface opens that shows a number of options through which you can keep your device maintained. Some of the major tasks that you can do are:

1) Backup - Taking a backup of your device so that your information is kept safe, and you get it back when you need it.

2) Update: The device will automatically check for any software updates of the device and will keep it running with the most recent features and security enhancements.

3) Sync: It synchronizes the device with the Mac, thus allowing the transfer of files, music, photos, and other content between these two devices.

4) Restore: Whenever necessary, return your device to the default settings or even to an earlier backup that may be helpful if you have any problems.

This makes it easy to keep your devices in sync and up to date without having to leave the Finder.

THE FINDER SIDEBAR

The Finder sidebar is one of the most important elements that will make the use of macOS much easier. On the left side of the Finder window is a sidebar that shows items you use regularly or want easy access to. This keeps everything nice and neatly organized for ease of file management.

Some of the important things that it usually contains in its sidebar include:

1) iCloud Drive: Once you click the iCloud Drive folder, you can see all of your documents that are stored in iCloud. Thus, it allows you to access those files kept in the cloud, making it very easy for you to work on a document from any of your other devices.

2) Shared Folder: This folder will show you documents you are sharing with others, as well as documents others are sharing with you. This is the best way to handle collaborative projects or access certain files from coworkers without having to search your entire file system.

To customize what appears in the sidebar, go to the top of the screen and select **Finder** > **Settings** from the menu. From the settings menu, you have the option to toggle on and off which items you want showing up in the sidebar, so that you can tailor it to your workflow and preference. This will keep some of your most used files and folders just a click away.

ADJUSTING FILE AND FOLDER VIEWS

macOS offers several methods to view files and folders in the Finder that you can use to select whichever you find most convenient and suitable for your needs. To change how you are viewing your documents and folders, locate the pop-up menu button at the top of the Finder window. The button opens a pop-up menu that allows you to choose any of several views:

1) Icon View ⊞: This view presents your files and folders as icons. It is an intuitive layout that immediately catches your eye, making it great for fast identification of files based on their visual appearance. Icon view is rather useful for image-containing folders, where icons will display thumbnails of your pictures.

2) List View ☷: This is a view in which the files and folders appear as a list. There are other details concerning this view, like the file size, date modified, and file type. In this kind of layout, it would be easy to sort out and manage your files, especially if you were dealing with many document files. Sorting of files in accordance with different attributes can be done by clicking on column headers.

3) Column View ⊞: This is a tree-like view that displays the contents of each folder in a separate column as one navigates through folders. So each time you select a folder, its contents open in another column. It's easy to drill into your directory structure and not get lost.

4) Gallery View ⊡: This is a visually rich layout showing an enlarged preview of the chosen file. For this reason, this view is perfect for detecting images and video clips, as well as other documents, very fast. From here, in the Gallery View you may also carry out all those fast changes

in the file, like rotate or mark up an image right within its preview.

Gallery View | Preview Pane

Scrubber bar | Combine PDFs, trim audio and video files, and automate tasks.

USING THE PREVIEW PANE

Of course, beyond just simple handling of files, there's one preference that you can turn on in Finder to make using it a bit easier: the ability to display the Preview pane. To do this, go under the menu bar and select View > Show Preview. By doing so, you will turn on a right-side panel in the Finder window that will provide additional information about the currently selected file.

To customize what displays in the Preview pane, based on the type of file you are working with, select View > Show Preview Options. You will now be able to select what options to display, saving you time by not having to open the actual file.

GALLERY VIEW

If you like to have the filename on the side of their respective files in Gallery View, turn this setting on. Press Command-J. This opens the view options. Then check the checkbox for Show filename, which adds the filenames underneath the previews. You still get to take advantage of having big visuals but can quickly identify what your files are.

QUICK ACTIONS

macOS introduced a feature with Gallery View and Column View called Quick Actions. These permit you to manage and edit files in the Finder without opening other applications. To access Quick Actions, click the button ⊙ at the bottom right of the Finder window.

Quick Actions give you access to a number of shortcuts which go a long way towards smoothing your productivity and workflow. A few of the things you can do include:

1) Rotate Images: It enables you to rotate images to your preferred orientation without necessarily opening an image editor.
2) Markup and Crop Images: You can markup or crop images right in the Finder by using the Markup tool. That's really useful when you just have a couple of quick edits you need to make.
3) You can combine the files; merging several images and PDFs into one single file. The documents or

presentations you will create will be well-organized.

4) Trim Audio and Video: You do have the capability with multimedia to trim audio and video without having to actually open an editing application; therefore, you have the capability of removing sections from the video or audio that you don't need.

5) Run Shortcuts: Get integrated productivity by running custom shortcuts you created in the Shortcuts app. That said, this feature gives you the ability to automate repetitive tasks right from Finder.

6) Automator Workflows: For power users, actions can also be created using Automator workflows. You might create an workflow that watermarks images or performs other bulk actions to files to help automate a process for you.

QUICK LOOK

Other powerful features in macOS include Quick Look. It allows you to view the contents of a file without having to open it completely. All you need to do to activate Quick Look is select a file in the Finder and press the Spacebar. You will instantly have a window open showing you what's inside the file.

In the Quick Look window's top, you have some buttons that you can click to:

1) Sign PDFs: While looking at a PDF, you can sign it right in the Quick Look interface without wasting extra time.

2) Trim Media Files: You can also trim audio and video files to your favorite length without leaving the Quick Look interface to do so.
3) Markup, Rotate and Crop Images: As in Quick Actions you can make basic adjustments to images - rotate or crop for example - directly in Quick Look.

ACCESSIBILITY TIP

If you have images and want to add an alternative description, you may easily do so; thus, making them much more accessible. Using Markup with either Preview or Quick Look, one can add a description-a much-needed feature that VoiceOver will be able to read for those users dependent on screen readers.

GET THERE FASTER WITH THE GO MENU

Finding your way into certain folders takes a number of clicks, but the Finder bar's **Go menu** can save you this hassle by easily accessing folders and locations. Here's how to make the most of it:
1) To get into common folders, like Utilities, all you have to do is go into the Go menu and click **Go > Utilities**. You won't need to click through several directories.
2) If you want to jump to the topmost level of nested folders, from here you can quickly go up along the folder hierarchy using Go > Enclosing Folder.
3) For a specific folder path, if you know exactly where you want to go, use Go > Go to Folder, then

simply type in the path. This allows you to go right to your destination in just a few keystrokes.

CHAPTER 7: THE DOCK ON YOUR MAC

The Dock is one of the most recognizable features in the Mac operating system, and it appears by default along the bottom of your screen. It's a good place to store those applications and documents you use most to help you work more efficiently and effectively. Here's a step-by-step guide on using the Dock to launch, switch between, and manage your applications and files.

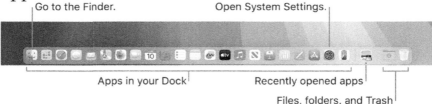

Go to the Finder.　　　　Open System Settings.

Apps in your Dock　　　　Recently opened apps

Files, folders, and Trash

HOW TO OPEN AN APPLICATION OR OPEN A FILE

The features of the Dock are that it provides quick access to applications; hence, it's easy to launch what you need without browsing through unnecessary navigation via menus or Finder windows. There are a couple of ways to open an app or file from the Dock:

1) Direct Click: To open an application, click on its icon in the Dock: every icon represents an application that opens an application directly.

2) Launchpad ⠿ : This is an icon in the bottom Dock; clicking on it will bring up a grid displaying all applications installed on your Mac. You scroll

through the icons and click to open any one of them.

3) Spotlight Search Q: For an even quicker way to find and open an app, use Spotlight Search. Located in the top right of the menu bar, click the magnifying glass icon or use the keyboard shortcut Command + Spacebar. Begin typing the name of the app you're looking for, and Spotlight will show relevant results. You can then select the app directly from the results to open it.

4) Recently Opened Apps: The center part of the Dock also shows your recently opened apps. This makes life even simpler because you can jump right back into applications you have opened recently, without searching for them.

CLOSING AN APP

Knowing how to correctly close an application is very critical when you want to manage system resources and maintain high performance. Here's how you can effectively close an app:

1) Close a window: The red dot in the top-left corner of an opened window will close it, but the application itself won't close. It's good for cleaning up your workspace without quitting the app.

2) Open Apps: Those applications which are currently opened can be identified by a little black dot beneath their icons in the Dock. This will show you that, though its window might be closed, the application is open.

3) Quit App: You quit an app to leave it completely shut and free up resources. To do this, control-click (or right-click) on its icon in the Dock. You see a context menu of options; choose Quit. This closes the application completely and removes it from active memory.

ADDING AN ITEM TO THE DOCK

You can add items in your Dock in order to customize it and make your work easier:
1) Drag and Drop:
    a) Locate the application, file, or folder you want to place in the Dock.
    b) Click and drag the item, holding it toward the Dock
2) Keep the item where you want to reside
    a) Apps: Dock them in the left area of the Dock. It is designed for applications where you can have access to your frequently used programs
    b) Files or Folders: Drag and drop these in the right area of the Dock. This space is allocated for various documents, folders, and other forms of files.
3) Release Item: Once you have dragged the item into place, release your mouse button or trackpad to let it drop into the Dock. The item will sit there in the dock for easy access to help with efficiency in your work.

REMOVING AN ITEM FROM THE DOCK

If you see that you no longer require the particular item in your dock then you can easily remove it:
1) Drag out of the Dock:
    a) Click and drag on the item you want to remove.
    b) Drag it out of the Dock and away from the icons.
    c) You will see a "Remove" label, indicating you can let go of the item.
2) Release the Item: When the item is outside the Dock, release the mouse button or trackpad. The item disappears from the Dock, but it isn't deleted from your Mac-the item is still available via Finder or Launchpad.

MISSION CONTROL: SEE EVERYTHING OPEN ON YOUR MAC

Mission Control is a mighty feature that helps you to see all the applications, windows, and desktops currently opened on your Mac for effective workspace management. Here's how you get the best out of it: 1. Accessing Mission Control: a. Keyboard Shortcut: The default shortcut of Mission Control is F3 or the icon of three rectangles 🖼 on the keyboard.
1) Trackpad Gesture: Perform a three-finger swipe upwards on the trackpad. This opens Mission Control, which gives a bird's-eye view of the applications and windows opened.
3. Navigate Open Windows:

a) Mission Control gives you a view of all opened windows, full-screen apps, and desktop spaces in one place.
b) This feature allows you to click on any window or app to immediately jump into it, smoothing out your workflow and enhancing multitasking.
4. Add Mission Control to the Dock:
   c) To have Mission Control easily at your fingertips, you'll want to add its icon to the Dock.
   d) To do so open Mission Control, and then open the Applications folder. Locate the Mission Control icon , and drag it onto the Dock placing it where you like on the Dock.

VIEWING ALL OPEN WINDOWS IN AN APP

Sometimes, you may have opened several windows in one application. Mac OS X makes it really easy to see what windows are open as well as switch between them:
1) Force Click on the App Icon:
   a) Locate in the Dock the app icon that has several windows opened.
   b) Force Click: This involves clicking on the app icon and pressing deeper in - or, in other terms, harder - on the trackpad or mouse. This will show you all the open windows of that application.

2) Switch Between Windows: Once you have this view, you can click any window to bring it forward to continue working with different windows without interruption.

CUSTOMIZING THE DOCK

You can personalize the appearance of the Dock in the following manner with macOS:

1) Open System Settings: From the top left corner of your screen, click the Apple menu and select System Settings.

2) Click Desktop & Dock: In this section, you will be able to adjust several visual and behavioral settings related to the Dock:

a) Size: This allows you to set the size bigger or smaller, depending on your preference. o Position: Move the Dock to the screen left or right side for a design you might find most appealing.

b) Hide Option: You can just set the Dock to hide when it is not being used; this may give you a neater working environment.

3) Changing the Magnification/ Minimized Windows Behaviour: You can easily change the magnification effects that come along with determining how the minimized window acts/behaves.

ADDITIONAL TIPS FOR USING THE DOCK

1) Changing Icons: The Dock is somewhat customizable, and one thing you can change is the icons on the Dock. Simply click and drag an app icon to the place in the Dock you want it to be. Release to set there.

2) Adding Applications: An application to be added to the Dock (in order to have fast access) must be located either in the Finder or Launchpad; afterward, click and drag it onto the Dock until it is dropped. Upon releasing it, the icon will stick to the Dock for easy opening the next time around.

3) Removing Applications: To remove an application from your Dock, click and drag the icon off of the Dock until you see a "Remove" label appear. Release the icon; it will disappear from the Dock without actually deleting the app itself.

4) Dock Preferences: You can open System Settings to alter the appearance and functionality of the Dock. You can change the size of the Dock, where it sits on the screen, and minimize window preferences within System Settings.

CHAPTER 8: NOTIFICATION CENTER ON YOUR MAC

The Notification Center is a single place that centralizes all your notifications and information you may want to access, such as calendar events, stocks, weather updates, and much more. This will keep you updated and informed without cluttering up the desktop with a number of app windows.

ACCESSING NOTIFICATION CENTER

You can access Notification Center by one of the following ways:
1) Clicking the Date or Time:
   a) The menu bar is usually located on the top right corner of your screen.
   b) Click the date or time that appears. Doing this will open the Notification Center where you will be able to see notifications and widgets.

2) Using a Trackpad Gesture: The more fluid gesture is the swiping left from the right edge of the trackpad with your two fingers. It opens the Notification Center, whereby you will have an easy and quick way to access notifications without getting out of your way of work.

3) Keyboard Shortcut: You can also use the F12 key or Control + Option + Command + D, depending on how your keyboard is set up to enable/disable the Notification Center.

4) Viewing Widgets: Once you open Notification Center, the top section is a list of notifications. Below these are several widgets that you can interact with. Scroll down to see more widgets and/or notifications as you would like to view.

INTERACTING WITH NOTIFICATIONS

The Notification Center is more than just a collection of passively displayed alerts; it is interactive and allows for quick actions:

1) Read Notifications: Notifications are stacked based on application, showing you the most recent alerts first. You will notice icons identifying the type of notification, such as Mail, Calendar, and Messages.

2) Take action Many notifications will offer choices to take action directly:

   a) Allowing/Responding to Emails: Often when receiving an email through notification, you can reply within the notification itself without having to open the Mail application. Click the notification to respond or use quick reply options.

   b) Managing Calendar Events: Click on a calendar notification so that you can view details about upcoming events; you can often add or modify events right from this view.

   c) Podcasts: When you get an alert saying a podcast has arrived, you can click or tap on it to begin listening right away, or you may view more details about the episode.

4. Viewing More Options:

   a) Click the arrow at the top-right of a notification to expand it. More options open to you on that notification, such as extra actions, links, or related settings.

b) For example, one may reply or mark the conversation as read by expanding the message notification.
5. Using Notifications on your iPhone: As with iPhone Mirroring, notifications from the iPhone can also pop up on the Mac. You can interact with the notifications right from the Mac by using Multitasking across devices. If you receive a text message on your iPhone, it will pop up on your Mac, and you can respond from there.

CUSTOMIZE NOTIFICATION PREFERENCES

You can further customize your Notification Center experience by adjusting notification settings for individual apps as follows:
1) Opening System Preferences: Click the Apple menu located at the top-left corner of your display, then select System Settings (or System Preferences, depending on your macOS version).
2) Selecting Notifications: Click on Notifications from the available choices. From here, you will have a list of all the apps that can show notifications.
3) Notification Settings: a. From the list, click any app to modify any settings related to notifications.
   a) Allow Notifications: ON/OFF to let/block notifications from that particular app.
   b) Alert Style: Choose how you want notifications to pop up in front of you, such as Banners, Alerts, or None.

c) Sounds: You can even set different sound options for receiving notifications from particular apps.

d) Notification Grouping: Choose whether notifications are kept grouped by apps or show up one by one.

4) Customizing Widgets: You can customize your Notification Center widgets. Where available, click the Edit Widgets button and drag-and-drop widgets to reorder them according to your needs. This allows you to keep the most important information at the top.

SETTING YOUR NOTIFICATION SETTINGS

The Notification Settings help you customize the kind of notifications you receive and how they should appear on your Mac, so you don't get distracted but still catch the important updates.

LAUNCH NOTIFICATION SETTINGS:

1) Open System Settings:
a) Click on the Apple menu located at the topmost part of your screen.
b) Click on System Settings (or click on System Preferences, depending on which one your OS shows).

2) Go to Notifications: Within the sidebar, find Notifications. This is where you choose how notifications appear and from which applications.

SETTING UP NOTIFICATIONS

Now that you are inside the Notifications window, let's look at configuring your settings to your liking:

1) Choose Applications: A list of applications that can show notifications will appear on the left-hand side. You can click on any one of these applications to configure its notification settings.

2) Notification Options: For each application, there are a number of settings you can modify:

   a) Allow Notifications: Allow or block notifications from that app.

   b) Alert Style: There are three different ways to present notifications:

      i) Banners: temporary notifications that appear along the top and automatically disappear.

      ii) Alerts: notifications that stick around until you take an action.

      iii) None: you won't see any notifications

   c) Notification Sounds: turn sounds for notifications from that app on or off.

   d) Badge App Icon: This will enable you to choose whether you have a red badge on the app icon showing notifications are unread.

   e) Show Previews: This option is where you can choose if you view notifications-Always, When Unlocked, or Never.

   f) Notification Grouping: This will bring up the choice of notification by application, automatic, or off.

3) iPhone Notifications

a) If you happen to use an iPhone, you can select to view iPhone notifications on your Mac. This is very helpful in keeping you connected without having to switch between devices.
b) Look for iPhone notifications in the Notifications settings and select the option to enable receiving alerts directly from your iPhone onto your Mac.

Conclusion

Notifications in macOS provide a quick way to stay organized and informed by managing your notifications, interacting with reminders, and showing you important information. You have learnt how to open it, interact with the notifications, and adjust its settings to improve productivity and enhance your experience on Macs.

FOCUS

This feature helps you in minimizing distractions and filtering notifications based on your current activity such as work, relax or focus on family. This feature helps you in staying focused on what is important at that moment.

SETTING UP FOCUS

1) Open Focus Settings: Open the System Settings menu and select Focus from the sidebar.
2) Choose one of the available options to enable Focus Mode:

a) Mac OS automatically provides you with some standard Focus modes, such as Do not Disturb, Personal, and Work; you can choose any of these or, if desired, create one.
b) To activate a focus mode, click on your preferred option.
3) Customize Settings for Focus:
a) You can tailor each Focus mode to allow notifications from certain apps or contacts. That is, while you may mute most notifications, you may want to allow critical alerts to come through from colleagues or family members.
b) Set up Focus for:
   i) People: Allow notifications from selected contacts-for instance, important calls or messages.
   ii) Apps: Enable notifications from selected apps you consider essential for your current activity.
   iii) Calls: Select to allow calls during your Focus time.
   iv) Time-sensitive notifications: Enable notifications which are marked as timesensitive to bypass the Focus setting.
4) Share Focus Across Devices: If you have several Apple device, then you can share your Focus status across devices. This includes the fact that when you turn on Focus on one device it will automatically turn on across devices for consistency.

5) Focus Filters: Apply Focus filters to block potentially distracting content from appearing within selected apps, such as Calendar and Messages. This helps you stay focused on the work at hand without additional distractions.

ENABLING AND DISABLING FOCUS

1) Quick Access:
   a) To turn Focus on and off quickly, click the Control Center icon ⊙⊙ - a pair of toggle switches - in the menu bar.
   b) Click the Focus section to open a list of available Focus modes, which you can enable.
   c) When Focus is on, Messages will display a status to your contacts that notifications are silenced. This way, others will know you are not available.
2) Set duration of Focus: Specify how long a Focus should be on, or turn it automatically on and off with the detection of location or time of day. Use this feature to keep up with the better balance in your work-life routine.

ACCESSING AND CUSTOMIZING YOUR WIDGETS

These are small applications that display information from your favorite apps right on your desktop or in Notification Center. You can make it your workspace by customizing them. They can display everything from the weather to Calendar events and reminders, among many other things. The following tutorial will explain how to add and remove widgets and rearrange them, including how to use widgets from your iPhone and third-party apps.

Step 1: Opening the Widget Gallery

1) Enter the Notification Center: Clicking the date and time in the the screen's upper-right corner opens the Notification Center. If you have a trackpad, you can also swipe left from the trackpad's right edge with two fingers.
2) Click Edit Widgets: At the bottom of the Notification Center, click on Edit Widgets. The widget gallery opens-that is, the view where available widgets are shown, organized by app.

Adding Widgets

1) Widget Gallery Browse: You scroll through the apps and available widgets in the gallery, for which you will notice the variations in the sizes and types depending on what's relevant in the functional knowledge of an app. Say, a weather app may allow small, medium, and large-sized widgets where it would show current conditions, forecasts, or alerts.
2) Add Widgets to Your Desktop:
   a) To add a widget, just click the widget size you want, and the widget will now appear inside your Notification Center. Drag and drop it onto the desktop if you prefer to get it outside of Notification Center.

b) Sing in with the same Apple ID to both your iPhone and Mac, you easily can add iPhone widgets to your Mac Desktop. Moreover, this will let you view lots of useful information without a need to install the corresponding apps on your Mac. Just find the widgets you have set up already on your iPhone.

3) Drag and Drop: Once added, the widget can be dragged to where you want it to sit in either the desktop or Notification Center. Place it where you can easily view it and arrange the layout to suit your workflow.

Step 3: Removing Widgets

1) Enter Edit Mode: Click again at the bottom of Notification Center to return to the Edit Widgets menu.

2) Remove Widgets:
   a) Locate the widget in the Notification Center which you'll like to remove. Click the minus (-) that shows up when you hover over it and the widget will disappear from your sight.
   b) When removing a widget, you aren't uninstalling the app but just concealing the widget from your desktop or Notification Center. You can add it any time later by returning to the widget gallery.

Step 4: Rearranging Widgets

1) Drag to Rearrange:

a) You can even reorder the widgets within the Edit Widgets mode. Click and drag any of the widgets to a new position, either within the Notification Center or on your desktop.

b) The widgets will snap into place so you can create a customized layout that prioritizes the information most important to you.

ADDING THIRD-PARTY WIDGETS

macOS also supports third-party widgets, which you can download from the App Store. These widgets will extend your desktop experience by offering added functionality that might not be available through the default macOS applications.

1) App Store: Open the App Store either from your Dock or through a Spotlight search by hitting Command + Space and typing "App Store".

2) Search for Widgets: Search for widget applications using the App Store's search or by heading to the "Widgets" category, if present. The trendy widget apps can give you options on how to manage your tasks, record fitness, or check more detailed weather.

3) Get the App Installed: Once you get your desired application offering widgets, click Get or Download to install it.

4) Add Third-Party Widgets: Now, to access Edit Widgets again, repeat the steps above. Now it will be in your widget gallery. Drag its widgets onto your desktop or to Notification Center like you would any other widget.

CUSTOMIZING YOUR WIDGETS TIPS

1) Mix and Match Sizes: Sometimes these variably-sized widgets will be capable of displaying variable amounts of information. You might make a few small, a few medium-sized, and a few large widgets in order to experiment with which you like best.

2) Group Similar Widgets: If you have a group of multiple widgets that all relate to similar information-say, calendar and reminders-you might want to group them together in such a way that a cohesive panel of information is presented.

3) Updates: From time to time, check for updates of those applications providing you with widgets. Developers might provide additional features or widgets that may be helpful.

4) Accessibility Features: Check, where available, the settings of your widgets if you have specific accessibility needs for color scheme and size preferences.

CHAPTER 9: ACCESSING CONTROL CENTER

The Control Center on your Mac puts frequently used settings in one easy-to-access place, right there in the upper right corner of the screen. That makes this even quicker because you will not have to navigate through several menus to adjust the settings you need. Instead, follow these steps:

OPEN CONTROL CENTER

To do so, click the Control Center icon 🎛 - it resembles two stacked switches - in the the menu bar's upper-right corner. This opens the Control Center panel, which includes most of your Mac's settings, arranged by category.

KEY FEATURES OF CONTROL CENTER

Once opened, you will notice that Control Center has a number of key controls in sections including:

BLUETOOTH AND WI-FI

1) Bluetooth:
   a) Bluetooth button: The Bluetooth button is used to enable or disable Bluetooth. Upon clicking the button, a drop-down menu appears displaying the connected devices and options available. You can connect or disconnect Bluetooth devices like headphones or mice here.
2) Wi-Fi:
   a) Click the Wi-Fi 📶 button to display all the available networks. From this menu, you can switch your network, view your preferred connections, and enter further options that concern Wi-Fi.
   b) You can also click on Open Wi-Fi Settings to dive deeper into the network configurations.

BRIGHTNESS AND VOLUME CONTROLS

1) Brightness: The Brightness slider controls screen brightness. This feature is handy when working with variable light conditions since you have a fast way to make changes without going through the display settings for changes.
2) Volume: The volume slider allows the adjustment of the audio output. Click the button for options to

adjust the system sound, and also controls for the connected audio devices.

ADDITIONAL OPTIONS

1) Click for More Options: There are numerous buttons in the Control Center that have more options upon a click. By clicking the Sound icon, for example, it can allow you to select audio output devices; you could switch from internal speakers, headphones, or external speakers.
2) Back to Main View: In the case of exploring extra options in the Control Center, clicking the icon of the Control Center ⬤ once more will take you back to its main view. Such a design keeps things hassle-free and speedy.

MASTERING YOUR DESKTOP WITH STAGE MANAGER

Along with the Control Center, another feature boosting your productivity by organizing your work area is Stage Manager.

WHAT IS STAGE MANAGER?

Stage Manager means the feature which lets you to automate the setup of your opened apps and windows. It will help organize your desktop better to focus on what is important for you at one moment but easily switch between applications.

1) Enable Stage Manager:
   a) To enable Stage Manager, open Control Center and tap the Stage Manager icon-it looks like a window with two other overlaid apps on top of one another. Tap to turn Stage Manager on.
   b) You can also enable it from the System Settings > Desktop & Dock; it has a toggle for Stage Manager.
2) Window Arrangement:
   a) Once Stage Manager is activated, open windows will align to the left-hand side of your screen. It keeps all your currently active applications in easy view without cluttering up your desktop with too many opened windows.
   b) Click any application from this list to make it the focus window; the other windows will remain partially visible at the side for easy switching between them.
3) Workspaces Creation
   a) You can also create custom workspaces by grouping related apps together. For example, if you are working on a presentation and want to refer to a document you will have both apps in one workspace. To group apps together you simply drag and drop them into the Stage Manager area.

MICROPHONE RECORDING INDICATOR

macOS includes a new built-in security feature that lets you know when your microphone is being used. It increases the sense of privacy and security by letting your view which applications are using your microphone.

APPEARANCE

When an application accesses the microphone, an on-record indicator - a small dot or an icon - appears at the top of the Control Centre. This may be helpful to ensure unauthorized applications without your knowledge cannot access your microphone.

INTERPRETING THE INDICATOR

An on-screen indicator is a good way to let you know when applications are currently using your microphone. If you happen to notice this 'on' indicator and happen not to be using an application that should have access to the microphone, it's probably a good idea to investigate further and know which application is making use of your microphone, with whatever action that warrants-quit the app, change permissions, etc.

MANAGE WHICH APPS CAN ACCESS THE MICROPHONE

To control permissions for what applications get to use your microphone, navigate to System Settings > Privacy & Security > Microphone. Here you'll be able to turn access off on a per-app basis, giving you more granular control of precisely which apps can use your microphone.

PINNING CONTROL CENTER FAVORITES

Control Center gives you fast access to settings of importance, and you could further your productivity by making sure your favorite things are pinned in the menu bar for even quicker ways of accessing them without having to always hover through the Control Center every time a setting change is needed.

1) Drag to Pin Favorites:
   a) To pin an item to the menu bar, click the icon on the upper right corner of your screen to open Control Center. Once open, locate your desired item to be pinned-example, Wi-Fi, Bluetooth, or Volume-and drag that icon into your menu bar at the top of your screen.
   b) When you release, it will pin the item into the menu bar for easy access.
2) Personalising Menu Bar:
   a) Adjust Menu Bar Items: In the System Settings, go to Control Center, where you can see all the items available in the Control Center.
   b) Choose "Show in Menu Bar" from the pop-up menu set beside each item. In this way, you will be able to enable different controls on and off to include only those that you will most likely need.

Choose additional modules
to add to Control Center.

3) Preview Item Placement: Within the same settings menu, a preview of where the control will appear in the menu bar is available. This feature ensures that the controls can be organized in a manner that makes sense for your workflow.

4) Limitations: Some items cannot be added or removed from the Control Center or to the menu bar. By nature, they limit functionality and security by possessing accesses to system-critical controls.

REMOVING ITEMS FROM MENU BAR

At one time or another, you may want to clean up your menu bar by removing things you either no longer use or need quick access to.

Quick Removal Process With the Command Key

1) To remove an item quickly from the menu bar, hit the Command key ⌘ on your keyboard. While holding the key click and drag the desired item from off the menu bar.

2) When you let go of the mouse button, the item will disappear from the menu bar; this, however doesn't mean it has disappeared for good as it's still available in the Control Center.

WHAT IS SPOTLIGHT?

Spotlight 🔍 is an integrated search utility in macOS that allows you to find documents, images, applications, emails, and more on your Mac with ease. It's designed to make access to information fast without having to go through numerous folders or applications.

OPENING SPOTLIGHT

Here's how to open Spotlight:

1) Using the Mouse: Click the Spotlight icon 🔍, a magnifying glass available inside the menu bar at your screen's top right.

2) Using the Keyboard:
   a) You can also use a keyboard shortcut for faster access. Press Command ⌘ + Space bar to open Spotlight. This is one of the fastest ways to initiate a search, and it's highly recommended if you want to be efficient.

b) Spotlight Key F4: With some keyboards, you may have a dedicated Spotlight key F4. Clicking this will also activate the Spotlight search field.

SEARCHING FOR ITEMS

Here are two ways of performing searches:

1) Type: Once you open the Spotlight 🔍, you can already begin typing what you are looking for. It will also show real-time results in Applications, Documents, Emails, Calendar Events, and Web Results as you type-on-the-go.

2) Live Text Feature: One of the useful things with Spotlight is that it allows you to search for text even within images. This is helpful, especially if what you want to find are screenshots of photos that have a written content. Note that this Live Text is available in some selected languages.

Start typing, and results appear quickly.

🔍 cooking

Photos From Apps   Show More >

Documents

The Recipe with Kenji and Deb
Deb Perelman & J. Kenji López-Alt

Related Searches

Search the Web

OPENING APPLICATIONS

Here are two ways of opening applications using Spotlight:

1) Type App Name: When you need to open an application, you only need to type the name in the search area of Spotlight. As an example, if you type "Safari", the Safari browser opens up.

2) Choose and Open: From the results of applications you've looked up, use Return to launch it instantly. You'll save your time rather than going through Applications or Launchpad yourself to open apps.

PERFORMING QUICK ACTIONS

Here are some tips for performing Quick Actions with Spotlight:

1) Launch Quick Actions: Besides searching for files or apps, Spotlight can also perform quick actions. You can use it to run shortcuts, toggle settings like Do Not Disturb on or off, and to set times and alarms.

2) Search for Actions: Open Spotlight and start typing what you want to do. For instance, if you type "Turn on Do Not Disturb", you'll find that option available to turn it on right from your search results.

3) Examples of Quick Actions: You can trigger the following system commands with typing:

   a) "Turn on Do Not Disturb" to toggle notifications off.

   b) "Set alarm for 7 AM" to set an alarm.

c) "Open System Preferences" to access immediate system settings.

TIPS FOR EFFECTIVE USE OF SPOTLIGHT

Here're are some tips for optimizing your Spotlight searches:

1) Refine Your Searches: If your search results are too broad, you can narrow them down by including specific keywords or by using filters. You could also try typing "Documents" after your search term.

2) Use Natural Language: Spotlight is designed to understand natural language queries. For example, you could type "Show me pictures from last summer" to find relevant images easily.

3) Access Web Results: Spotlight can pull in results from the web, in addition to local files and applications, making it a very useful option for quick searching online.

4) Set up Spotlight Preferences: Configure Spotlight to your advantage, open the System Settings > Siri & Spotlight. You can select here which categories of indexing and displaying Spotlight shall be allowed to perform. This will make you focus more on relevant search results.

CURRENCY, TEMPERATURE AND MEASUREMENT CONVERSIONS

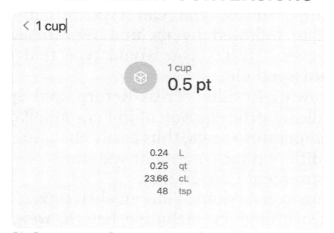

1. Spotlight can be quite handy in converting currencies without necessarily opening a separate converter application or going online to get conversions. Here's how you can use it effectively;

   a) Enter the Currency: Just type in the currency sign then the amount you want to be converted. Suppose you want to convert $100 into euros, you will type into "$100" in Spotlight and hit Return.

   b) View Converted Values: Spotlight displays a table with different values of the amount specified and it will be listed across various forms of currency. This feature will save you time from surfing the web by giving you the current conversion rates at your fingertips.

   c) Examples: Typing in "€50" will generate its equivalent in other currencies, such as dollars and yen.

3. Temperature Conversions:
   a) Temperature Conversion: To convert temperatures, you can type a temperature value followed by its unit. For instance, to convert "32°C", you would type that directly into Spotlight.
   b) Viewing Results: Press Return, and Spotlight will show the equivalent in Fahrenheit or other temperature units, thus easily changing over to a different measurement system.
4. Measurement Conversions:
   a) Unit Conversions: You can also convert various measurements, including length, weight, and volume. In doing so, you will type the type of measurement you wish to convert, the amount, and the unit it is currently in. Example: If you type "10 miles to kilometers," it will return the number after it has been converted.
   b) Examples: To convert "5 liters to gallons," you would type that into Spotlight, and it will return the amount in gallons.

NARROWING YOUR SEARCH

Spotlight is configured to deliver a wide scope of results, but sometimes you want to refine the search term to be more specific: That is by narrowing, exclusion of specific folders, disks, and information types like emails or text messages. This becomes helpful in case you have volumes of data and want to situate yourself to particular areas.

1) Accessing Search Settings: To change these defaults open System Settings, then select Spotlight. Once in this menu you want to select Search Results.
2) Choosing Categories: Once you're in this menu you'll be able to choose categories. For example if you don't like for Spotlight to go searching for Messages or Mail you'd de-select those options.
3) Advantages: The advantages here are that you can have much "cleaner" searches, seeing only what you are looking for.

USING SIRI SUGGESTIONS

Siri Suggestions is part of Spotlight and refines the search by offering contextually relevant information from all types of sources, including but not limited to:
1) What is Siri Suggestions? These are suggestions that draw information from sources such as Wikipedia, web searches, news articles, sports updates, weather forecasts, stocks, and movies.
2) How to Turn On Siri Suggestions: As soon as you start typing into Spotlight, related Siri Suggestions appear right in your search results for quick access to even more.
3) Search Information: For example type "weather," and Siri Suggestions may show you the current weather in your location, or various links about weather-related websites, news about weather events from around the world.
4) Constrain Siri Suggestions: If you would prefer Spotlight search only focus on things you have

stored on your Mac, you can disable Siri Suggestions. For this, open the System Settings, click Spotlight and under Search Results uncheck the check box next to Siri Suggestions. This will ensure Spotlight will only show local files and applications in your search results.

SETTING UP SIRI

1) Open System Settings: Click the Apple menu at the top-left corner of the screen. Find the System Settings option there, but if working with a pre-2019 version of macOS, click the System Preferences instead. That would be used for altering several settings available on Mac.
2) Access Siri Settings: In the System Settings window, choose Siri & Spotlight from inside the sidebar. Here, all the Siri settings are housed.
3) Enable Siri: Find the **Enable Ask Siri** check box and click on it to enable Siri. This check box needs to be ticked. Now Siri will be ready for your orders.
4) Confirmation: After you turn Siri on, you might be prompted to confirm the action. Select the **Enable** Button to confirm the enabling.
5) Set up Siri preferences: Once you have turned Siri on, you can further edit several settings in order to personalize Siri as per your need:
   a) Language: Click the pop-up menu beside Language to choose the language you want Siri to use for responses and interactions. Siri is

capable of using many languages. Please choose suitable for you.

b) Voice: Select Voice from the Voice settings, and then select one of Siri's voices. You can choose between different accents and genders to your liking.

c) Show in Menu Bar - If you want immediate access to Siri right from the menu bar, then select this check box to show Siri there. The option means that every time you want to use Siri, you can click on the Siri icon at any moment in case you don't want to use a voice prompt.

6) Using the Dictation/Siri Key: If you're using a Magic Keyboard that has a Touch ID button, you can quickly access Siri using the F5 key 🎤 (which also functions as Dictation or Siri button) on your keyboard. This is a quick alternative to voice activation.

7) Setting Up Voice Activation: To activate Siri using your voice you may say "Hey Siri," or "Siri." To set this up:

a) Select the System Settings again, then click on the Siri & Spotlight option.

b) Find the option that says **Listen for** and click the associated pop-up menu. Here you can select either use Hey Siri or just Siri.

c) Follow On-Screen Instructions: Once you have chosen to turn voice activation on, you will be taken through a set-up process, including perhaps repeating a few phrases to help Siri recognize your voice and fine-tune its accuracy.

TURNING ON SIRI

1) Turn on Siri: After setting up Siri in the System settings, there are multiple ways to turn it on, making it very easy to access:

   a) Keyboard shortcut: Press the Command ⌘ and Space bar keys together. This is a fast shortcut to invoke the Siri:

   b) Menu Bar Icon: If you have set it to appear in the menu bar, you'll click on the Siri icon ⚫ at the top right of your screen that looks like a little waveform or a little circle. This approach will be useful for those of you who like to see it to click it.

   c) Voice Activation: If you have enable the feature "Hey Siri," you can say it: "Hey Siri" to immediately access Siri. It is a good hands-free option to multitask or when both of your hands are busy doing something else.

2) More About Siri: To learn more things Siri can do, say, "What can you do?" A list of the things Siri can do will appear. You can also go to the Apple website: Apple.com/siri for detailed information about Siri.

3) Type to Siri: If you don't wish to talk to Siri or you are in a surrounding that has high levels of noise, you can type your request.

   a) Activate Siri: Tap the Siri icon inside the menu bar. Alternatively, press hot keys Function (Fn) or Globe key 🌐 + S to turn on Siri.

   b) Typing Your Command: Once Siri is activated, you will encounter the Siri interface where you can type what you want to ask or order. This facility will be useful for those users who do not want to speak the command or those who have hearing impairments.

4) Show Captions: To hear and improve accessibility for what Siri is responding to, turn on the captions:

   a) Open System Settings from the Apple menu in the top-left corner of your screen. Note: In newer macOS versions, this is labelled as System Settings; on older versions, it's System Preferences.

   b) Select Siri & Spotlight in the sidebar.

   c) Enable Captions: Under the Siri Responses section, make sure there is a check next to

"Always show Siri captions." This means every response that Siri says will also be written on your screen for you to read.

5) Customize Siri Voice: In this section, learn how to change your Siri Voice settings:
   a) Open Siri Settings: Go back to System Settings and click on Siri & Spotlight.
   b) Siri Voice Selection: Locate the menu called Siri Voice. You will see voice variants, each different from others with regard to accent and gender. Tap the dropdown to listen to the different voices.
   c) Voice Options: Depending on what OS you are running, you may have a few voice options on your Mac. You can choose to have Siri to use another language, accent, or even a different gender. Choose your favorite and from that point forward, that is how Siri will sound.

USING SIRI FOR EVERYDAY TASKS

Siri can assist you in almost everything, from the simplest to the most complex tasks. Following are some of the very helpful voice commands you may want to use:

1) Events Scheduling and Management:
   a) Calendar Management: You easily set up meetings or create reminders. You could say for example:
   Siri: "Create a new meeting for tomorrow at 2 PM."
   Siri: "Add a reminder to call Mom at 5 PM."

144

b) Checking Your Calendar: To check upcoming events, just ask:
Siri: "Show me my calendar for this week."

2) Finding Information:
a) General Queries: For anything you want to know, Siri can answer it. Example:
Siri: "How high is Mount Whitney?"
Siri: "What time is it in Paris?"
b) Navigational Assistance: If you are wondering how to get somewhere, you can say:
Siri: "How do I get home from here?" Siri will give you directions using Apple Maps.

3) Messaging and Calls:
a) Messaging: Siri can save you from hassle in sending a text or message; it's as simple as:
Siri: "Send a message to John saying I'll be late."
b) Calling: You can also make calls with Siri:
Siri: "Call Mom" or "FaceTime Sarah."

MORE EXAMPLES OF SIRI COMMANDS

Here are more examples that will inspire your usage of Siri:

1. **General Questions:**
Siri: "What's the weather like today?"
Siri: "How tall is the Eiffel Tower?
Siri: "Tell me a joke."

2. **Productive Tasks:**
Siri: "Create a new note."
Siri: "Remind me to call Mom at 3 PM."
Siri: "Show me my reminders."

3. **Navigation and Directions:**

Siri: "Directions to the nearest coffee shop."
Siri: "How do I get to the office?"
4. **Media Control:**
   Siri: "Play some music."
   Siri: "Pause video."
   Siri: "What's the latest news?"
5. **Device Control:**
   Siri: "Turn on Do Not Disturb."
   Siri: "Dim the brightness to 50%."

DRAWBACKS AND REMARKS

1. Internet Connectivity: Siri will only work on Mac if it has access to the internet. It is through the internet that Siri pulls information, answers questions, and executes commands.
2. Language and Regional Availability: Remember that Siri is not available in all languages and in all regions, and some of its features may be enabled only in certain parts of the world. So, if you try something and it doesn't work, check to see whether Siri supports this command in your native language.

TROUBLESHOOTING SIRI

In case of any issues related to Siri:
1) Check Internet Connection: o Siri is an Internet-based assistant. Ensure that your Mac is connected to Wi-Fi.
2) Microphone Issues: Verify the microphone of your Mac. Do this by attempting other voice input features or applications.

3) Privacy Settings: If Siri does not respond to voice command, check your microphone privacy settings through System Settings under Privacy & Security.

CHAPTER 10: GIVING YOUR IMAC SOME PERSONALITY

That is because the personalization of your iMac is going to introduce more comfort into the area you are sitting in and working with, along with a touch of uniqueness. This lesson will reveal how to change the wallpaper, attach widgets, and make your desktop look exactly the way you want it to be.

HOW TO CHANGE THE WALLPAPER

Changes in wallpaper are among the easiest ways to give your iMac a fresh look:

1) Open System Settings: Click the Apple menu at the upper-left corner of your screen and then select System Settings, or System Preferences, based on your macOS version.
2) To get to Wallpaper: In the system settings sidebar, select Wallpaper. The window for setting wallpaper opens.
3) Select Your Wallpaper You will see some default wallpapers provided by Apple, or click **Desktop Pictures** to browse through a lot of categories.
4) To use a personal photo, click the Photos folder in the left sidebar to select an image from your library. Or, navigate to any specific folders where you store your images.
5) Select Wallpaper Style: Select the wallpaper to use with options like static or to dynamically change at set intervals such as every hour or day.

6) Match Your Screensaver: If you want everything to match, you could use the same picture for your wallpaper and your screensaver. You can also do this through Screensaver settings, which is still under System Settings.

7) Set the Wallpaper: Once you have your choice, click out of the settings. Your new wallpaper will take effect and give your desktop a new refreshed personal look.

ADD WIDGETS TO YOUR DESKTOP

Widgets put key information and apps in view to make your desktop more functional and personalized to your needs. To do this, follow these steps:

1) Open Notification Center: Click the date or time in your screen's upper-right corner to open the Notification Center. This is where you can access notifications and widgets.

2) Add Widgets: To add a widget to Notification Center, click Add Widget at the bottom. This

opens the Widget Gallery where you can see several widgets that you can use on your desktop.

3) Widget Options: You shall be able to look at different types of widgets for addition, including:
   a) Photos: There you can put a photo widget inside, showcasing particular album photos or memories.
   b) Podcasts: A Podcast widget can let you know where you left off with your favorite shows and episodes.
   c) Calendar: Events widget will show what's next.
   d) Weather: You can add a weather widget that will show current conditions and forecasts.
4) Add and Rearrange Widgets:
   a) To add a widget, just click on it or drag it into Notification Center or to your desktop.
   b) You can reorder widgets by dragging them onto your desktop or into the Notification Center.
5) Making Widget Size Changes: Most widgets come in a number of different sizes, including small,

medium, and large. Frequently you'll be able to click and hold on a widget to show resize options where that makes sense for you and is supported on your screen.

6) Removing Widgets: To remove a widget from Notification Center if you no longer want it: Click and hold, then click Remove Widget or drag outside Notification Center.

CUSTOMIZE YOUR DESKTOP ENVIRONMENT

Further customization of the desktop may involve:

1. Changing Desktop Icons: You can customize the icons of folders and applications on your desktop. Once you right click on the icon of your folder or application, select Get Info, then drag in an image onto the icon box to change it to the custom icon.

2. Organize Desktop Items: Create files and applications with folders. Right-click the desktop, then select New Folder. Identify the folder by file type stored inside it. Drag relevant items into that folder to keep the desktop clean.

3. Dock Settings: There are those things you cannot live without in your interface: The Dock. You can change its position - bottom, left or right side of the screen - or even its size from System Settings > Dock & Menu Bar. Consider enabling Magnification to make icons larger when hovering over them.

4. Create Stacks: macOS offers you Stacks, which enable you to clean up the files on your desktop.

Right-click the desktop and click "Use Stacks." This will then organize similar files (e.g., documents, images, etc.) into stacks, which allows for tidier desktops.

CREATE A MEMOJI ON MACOS

One fun thing you can do on a Mac is creating a Memoji. As a matter of fact, that's pretty easy, and for many, that may be an exciting way to visually express themselves in messaging and other platforms. That means toning skin, to accessories, creating a Memoji image that is specifically you. Your Memoji adds an original touch and makes your experience of macOS really personal. It can be used as an account picture, in messaging apps, or even on the log-in screen. Here is an inclusive guide on how to create and customize your Memoji, which will make it yours.

1) Open System Settings: First, you need to get into the System Settings to start creating your Memoji:
   a) Opening the Apple Menu: Click on the Apple logo at your screen's top left.
   b) Choose System Settings: In the menu that drops, click on System Settings-or if you're using an older macOS version, it will say System Preferences.
2) In System Settings, go to **Users & Groups**: Now that you are inside the System Settings, scroll down the sidebar of System Settings and click Users & Groups. This area deals with your user accounts and settings.

3) Choose a Profile Picture: You are now in the Users & Groups. Next to your login name, you will find your current profile picture. Tap this image to make changes to it.
4) Click Memoji: When the pop-up menu opens, you will have a number of options for changing your picture: Tap on **Memoji**. This will then open the Memoji creation interface.
5) Create Your Memoji: Since you have now opened the Memoji interface, you can go ahead to create your personalized emoji:
   a) Click the Plus Sign (+): To start creating a new Memoji, click on the plus sign. This will launch a set of customization options where you can design your Memoji.
   b) Personalize Your Memoji: You will be given a set of options to make a personalized Memoji. Some of the options you can personalize are:
      i) Skin Tone: You can choose from a wide range of skin tones that are pretty much close to your look.
      ii) Hairstyle: There, you will get an option to select different lengths and color of hairstyle. You can try different versions until you create one that accurately represents you.
      iii) Eyes: You can change the shape, color, and even add lashes to your Memoji's eyes if you want to give it a bit of personality.

iv) Nostrils and Mouth: You get to choose nose shapes and colors of lips for finer details of your Memoji's face.

v) Ears: Choose the ears' shapes and sizes that actually match yours.

vi) Facial Hair: If you have some facial hair, then you could add mustaches, beards, and goatees, too, along with their colors.

vii) Headwear: Go ahead to check out options for hats, eyeglasses, and more to complete your look.

viii) Accessories: You can add unique accessories to your Memoji, such as earrings or sunglasses, to make it really different.

6) Preview Your Memoji: As you change your Memoji, a live preview of your creation will show up on screen. This is how you know exactly how every edit affects your Memoji in real time.

7) Save Your Memoji: Once you are satisfied with the design of your Memoji, tap Done. Your Memoji is saved now and ready for use.

8) Making your Memoji your Profile Picture: Once you've saved your Memoji, now you can set it as your profile picture:

a) Select Your Memoji: You can see your newly created Memoji in the options of your picture in the Users & Groups settings again. Tap on it to set it as your profile image.

9) Using Your Memoji Across Apps: Now that your Memoji is ready, you can use it across apps like this:

a) Apple Account Picture: Your Memoji will appear as an Apple account picture whenever you sign in using your Apple ID to any device or service.
b) Contacts: You can set your Memoji in the "My Card" section in the Contacts app to identify yourself easily for others.
c) Messaging and FaceTime: With Messages and FaceTime, use your Memoji to chat with friends and make video calls, putting a personal touch.
d) Login Window: The Memoji will appear on the login screen to pictorially represent you at Mac startup.

CHAPTER 11: WORKING WITH MULTIPLE SPACES ON MAC

To have maximum productivity in Mac, good management of your workspace is necessary. Though creating multiple desktops is certainly one of the most productive ways, managing them becomes more flexible through Mission Control, where created desktops are referred to as 'spaces'. It lets you arrange your opened windows and apps better, avoiding clutter and helping to focus on particular tasks. A step-by-step detail on how to create and manage spaces in a Mac is shown below.

1. UNDERSTANDING MISSION CONTROL

Mission Control is a powerful feature in macOS that gives you an overview of all your open windows, desktops, and full-screen apps. It lets you rapidly move between different spaces and manage your workspace more effectively.

2. ENTERING MISSION CONTROL

To create and manage spaces, first, you have to enter Mission Control. There are a couple of ways you could do this:

1) Using a Trackpad: Three-finger swipe up on your trackpad-a gesture that opens Mission Control, showing you all your open windows and spaces.
2) Use keyboard: Mission Control key, usually F3 or a key showing three rectangles, or press Control +

Up Arrow. This too takes you into Mission Control.

The Spaces bar

Create a space.

Desktop   Calendar   Photos & Mail

Access full screen or Split View apps.

3. CREATING A NEW SPACE

Spaces let you organize your opened applications and windows into separate desktops so that you can focus on specific tasks without visual clutter. When you are in Mission Control, you can simply create a new space:

1) The Spaces Bar: There, you will see the Spaces bar at the top of your screen displaying thumbnails of your desktops and full-screen apps currently running.

2) Click the Plus (+) Button: Locate the plus sign (+) on the right-hand side of the Spaces bar. Clicking that button creates a new space. You can create up to 16 spaces.

3) Finish Creating Your Spaces: When you click the plus button, a new space will pop up. This will reflect in the Spaces bar, where you can immediately have its thumbnail shown.

4. SWITCH BETWEEN SPACES

Once you have configured an area, it is relatively easy to switch between desktops in the following way. To switch between desktops:

1) Click the Space Thumbnail: In the Spaces bar, click on any one of the space thumbnails that you want to open. It will open up the view of that particular space.

2) Swipe between Spaces: Or if you are more into gestures, you can switch across your created spaces by swiping over the trackpad leftwards or rightwards using three fingers.

5. WORKING IN A SPACE

Working on a space, you would only see the opened windows and applications of that specific space; hence, your workflow would remain neat and clean and wouldn't get disorganized/disrupted by other opened applications.

6. CONFIGURING EACH SPACE

In order to make different spaces more personalized and thus easily distinguishable, you can assign different desktop pictures to each:

1) Set Wallpaper for All Desktops: Open System Settings: click the Apple menu, then select System Settings, or System Preferences. Under the Desktop & Screen Saver, you choose a wallpaper for all spaces.

2) Change Wallpaper for Individual Spaces: Go to Mission Control and switch to whatever space you want. Right-click on the desktop to select Change Desktop Background. Choose a different wallpaper for that space. Do this with each space if you want to establish a different look for them.

7. MANAGING SPACES

As your workflow changes, you may want to rearrange or remove spaces in any of these following manners:

1) Rearranging Spaces: In the Spaces bar, click and drag a space's thumbnail left or right to rearrange the order of your spaces.
2) Removing a Space: To delete a space, enter Mission Control, hover over the space you want to remove, and click the "X" that appears in the corner of the space thumbnail. This will delete that space.

DIFFERENT WAYS TO SWITCH BETWEEN SPACES ON MAC

Switching between spaces on your Mac can make a big difference in how much work you get done, just by organizing your workspace. From Trackpad gestures to keyboard shortcuts and the Touch Bar, macOS offers a few ways to move around among multiple desktops with ease. These include the following:

1. TRACKPAD GESTURES

Your trackpad is multi-touch enabled, and this allows you to have some pretty natural gestures to move between spaces with ease. Here's how you do this:

1) Three-finger swipe-on most MacBooks and other trackpads, swiping left or right with three fingers will take you between spaces. This saves time because you won't be interrupting whatever you may be doing.
2) Four-Finger Swipe: Depending on your trackpad settings, you might also use a four-finger swipe to do this. This can be set in System Settings > Trackpad under the More Gestures tab. Use whichever is most comfortable to you.

2. USING A MAGIC MOUSE

Using a Magic Mouse is quite straightforward. You can easily move from one space to the other by performing simple gestures. These are:

1) Swipe with Two Fingers: Place two fingers on the Magic Mouse and swipe left or right to switch between spaces. This gesture emulates using a trackpad-swipe gesture and will smoothly transition between your organized workspace.

3. USING KEYBOARD SHORTCUTS

For those who are accustomed to-or merely partial to-keyboard control, macOS makes it quite easy to use keyboard shortcuts to navigate through spaces:

1) Control Key with Arrow Keys: Press and hold the Control key, then tap the Right Arrow key to head to the space on the right or the Left Arrow key to go to the space on the left. This is quite fast and efficient, especially when switching between spaces very often.

4. USING MISSION CONTROL

Mission Control provides an overview of all your opened windows and open spaces for easy navigation and management of your workspace. Following are some of the ways to manage the Mission Control application:

1) Entering Mission Control: To enter Mission Control, you have three options: you may swipe upwards with three fingers on your trackpad, hit the Mission Control key typically the F3, or click Control and the Up Arrow. After selecting Space via the Spaces Bar,

2) Once in Mission Control, move your cursor to the top edge of the screen, where you will see the Spaces bar. On the Spaces bar, you will see a thumbnail of all the active open spaces.

3) Click the thumbnail of the space you would like to switch to. This is pretty useful if you have many open spaces and you want an overview of them before selecting one.

5. USING THE TOUCH BAR (FOR MACBOOK PRO MODELS)

If you have a MacBook Pro with a Touch Bar, you can easily switch spaces using it:

1) Enable with Touch Bar: To be able to see your spaces in the Touch Bar, you first have to enable that option. Open System Settings and go to **Keyboard** and then select the option to show spaces in the Touch Bar.

2) Tap to Switch Spaces: When the feature is activated, the Touch Bar will show you thumbnails of your active spaces. Tap on the space you want to open and immediately get switched into that desktop.

TIPS FOR SPACES USE

1) Keep it tidy: If you create so many spaces too frequently, then regular clean-up of those you don't use may keep the Spaces bar from cluttering and slow navigation.

2) Direct attention to specific tasks: Applications concerning one form of work must be opened within the same space. For instance, all design applications may be on one space, and all research ones on another. This simply said, will reduce the number of times you have to switch between spaces.

3) Employ full-screen apps: In case you are working with full-screen applications like Safari or your design program, they will automatically create a

new space. This too can be leveraged for minimizing distractions.

4) Practice Gesture Control: Familiarize yourself with the gestures for switching spacing in lightning speed with your trackpad or Magic Mouse. With more practice, it surely will become second nature.

5) Customize Settings: Go to System Settings > Trackpad or Mouse, where you can adjust the sensitivity to your liking and enable or disable certain gestures.

That's part of the beauty of Spaces in macOS: you can dictate that specific apps will always open in certain spaces. This cleans up your workflow by decreasing distractions, and everything is exactly where you expect it each time. Let's go through the process step-by-step, covering each of the options available as you assign apps to spaces.

HOW TO ASSIGN APPS TO SPACES ON MACOS STEP BY STEP

1) Open the App you want:
   a) The first thing you do is fire up an application you would like to attach to a particular space. An already opened application will be shown in the Dock.
   b) Locate its icon in the Dock. Control-click or right-click the app icon to open a menu list of options.

2) Click 'Options' then Choose an 'Assign To' Option: Hover over Options in the menu, and you will see

a number of options appear under Assign To. You have a few configuration options; here each is a different way to handle managing your application's location across spaces:

1) All Desktops:
   a) All Desktops: It selects all the desktops and opens the application in every space that you have created. This is useful for applications that might be needed whatever the workspace context, such as communication applications like Messages or Slack and productivity applications like Calendar or Reminders.
   b) Opening the app in every space means its windows will follow you when switching between spaces, hence reducing the need to toggle between different screens.
2) This Desktop:
   a) Choose This Desktop keeps the application in the current space. Every time you open this application, by default it opens in this space alone.
   b) The option is pretty handy for task-related applications. You might want to keep design tools like Adobe Photoshop or Illustrator in one space while your coding tools are in Xcode or Terminal in another space.
   c) If you have selected full-screen for the app to open, then it opens a space unto its own in that desktop that you choose.

3) Desktop on Display [Number]:
   a) If you are working with more than one display then macOS allows you to assign an app to a particular display for a specific desktop. It will be labeled Desktop on Display [number] in the menu where each external monitor or built-in display has been assigned a different number.
   b) This option is useful in dual-display setups where you'd want a video call app, say, always on Display 1, and a presentation tool open on Display 2, each confined to their spaces for easy access and maximum use of screen estate.
4) NONE:
   a) Choosing None clears any space assignment for the application. That is to say, the application will open in whatever space you happen to be using. If you don't need to have a particular workspace configuration, this keeps things flexible and allows the application to open wherever you may happen to be.
   b) NONE - Apps are best designated for applications that are occasional-use only. It would be irrelevant to give a specific space designation for system utilities or to productivity applications that see very little use.

MORE TIPS TO MANAGE APP BEHAVIOR IN SPACES

1) Automatic Switching to a Space with an Already Open Window:

a) By default, if you switch into an application, macOS automatically switches to the space where an already open window of that app resides. This default behavior is pretty useful when you want to avoid opening a duplicate window and jumping between spaces.

b) For example, if you have a document open in **TextEdit** in Desktop 3 and then click to create a new TextEdit window in Desktop 2, macOS will whisk you back to Desktop 3 where the open windows are already showing.

2) System Settings: How to Customize This Behavior

a) To change this behavior, open the Apple menu and click System Settings. Click **Desktop & Dock** in the sidebar and scroll down to Mission Control. Go to the option for Moving to a Space where the application's windows are open when you want to switch apps.

b) You can turn this on and off as you please. Off continues to open a new app window in your current space, which is great if you like to keep workspaces strictly separated.

PRACTICAL APPLICATIONS OF ASSIGNING APPS TO SPACES

App assignment to spaces can be used to extend productivity by offering a clean, separated space for related tasks. This is for focused and segregated task separation in work environments. The given scenarios are quintessence use of the feature for the following:

1) Focus and Task Segregation: Assign the productivity apps-Word and Excel-to one space, creative apps like Photoshop and Illustrator to another, and comms apps like Slack or Zoom to a third. In this way, you will be able to enter the appropriate space depending on the task at hand, helping you with focused work without clutter in the mind.

2) Multiple Display Setups: Assign certain apps to specific desktops on certain displays, especially for users with dual or triple monitor setups. Examples might include reserving Display 1 for project management apps, Display 2 for coding or content creation, and Display 3 for web browsing or research.

3) Entertainment and Break Spaces: Or make a space dedicated only to non-work applications: music, video sharing sites, news sites, whatever. Then, when you feel like taking a break, switch to the 'entertainment' space without fiddling with your main workspaces.

MOVING AN APPLICATION WINDOW FROM ONE SPACE TO THE OTHER

Working with more than one space open in macOS, each can be dedicated to certain tasks or workflows, the capability of moving windows across is priceless to adapt to the priorities that change. There are two basic ways to transfer app windows from one space to the other.

METHOD 1: DRAGGING TO THE EDGE OF THE SCREEN

4) Select the App Window to Move: Click and hold down on the title bar of the window of the application you want to move.
2. Drag to Screen's Edge: With the window of the application held, drag it to either the screen's left or right edge. After a short while, macOS will automatically bring the window into the next adjacent space in that direction.
3. Continue to Adjacent Spaces:
    a) To take it further, pull the window to the screen's edge until you reach where you would want to create space.
    b) Practical Use Case: This is helpful if you have, for example, moved windows between spaces in succession-for instance, taking a project management application to a workspace closer to your current space.

METHOD 2: MOVING WINDOWS VIA MISSION CONTROL

1) Access Mission Control:
    a) Three-finger swipe up on trackpad, using Mission Control key-F3-on keyboard, or Control-Up Arrow shortcut.

b) In Mission Control, there is a Spaces bar right across your screen's top with thumbnails of each space.
2) Drag and Drop the Window: Locate the window of the app you want to move in the active space section and drag it to any other space in the Spaces bar.
3) Put Windows in Split View:
   a) If you drag the app window onto the full-screen app thumbnail, macOS will automatically place the two apps in Split View within that space so that you can work with them side by side.
   b) Practical Use Case: You will want to use this approach when you're moving around between several window reorganizations or navigating between distantly placed spaces. This is because Mission Control gives an overview of all your spaces and all open windows.

DELETING A SPACE

If you no longer need a certain space, you are able to easily delete it, which might help clean up your workspace from clutter. Performing the deletion of a space on macOS is pretty easy, though for that you need access to Mission Control.
1) Enter Mission Control: To open Mission Control, use any of the following: three-finger swipe upwards on the trackpad, Mission Control key (F3), or Control-Up Arrow.

2) Go to the Spaces Bar: At the top of the screen, thumbnails of each open space appear; this is called the Spaces bar.

3) Select the Space You'd like deleted: Pass the cursor over the space you'd like to have deleted, and an "X" icon will appear in the corner of that thumbnail.

4) Delete the Space: Once you clicked the "X" to delete the space: the open windows of that space automatically will move into another space. Hence you will never lose access to any of your files or applications.

5) Real-world Application: You would want to delete a space when you want to go back to having fewer workspaces once for example you have finished a project so you don't have a cluttered interface.

EXITING FULL-SCREEN OR SPLIT VIEW IN SPACES

Sometimes you want to remove an application from full screen or Split View, but not the space itself. To leave full screen or Split View places that app back into a windowed mode in the current space.

1) Enter Mission Control: Open Mission Control using one of the methods outlined above.

2) Hover Over the Full-Screen or Split View Thumbnail: Find the full screen or Split View thumbnail for the application in the Spaces bar.

3) Exit the Full-Screen or Split View Mode:

a) Move the cursor onto the image in the thumbnail until you see an Exit button ⤢ , click that. This will shut the full-screen mode down and send the app back into its normal window in the space.
b) Practical Use Case: this is useful if you want to quickly switch an app to windowed mode to multitask with other apps while still having them stay in the same space.

BEST PRACTICES FOR MANAGING SPACES

You can work much more productively with macOS if you effectively use and handle the spaces. Here are a few tips to help you keep your workspace organized and productive:

1) Plan Your Spaces by Task or Project: Create different spaces for different tasks that you do, like work, personal, study, etc., and that way you can keep yourself focused on your current work. Create related apps in every space so you can easily shift between a really focused environment without being distracted by unrelated apps or files.

2) Limit the Number of Spaces: While macOS supports up to 16 spaces, too many of them will make it a nightmare to remember where everything is. Stick to not having more than you actually need at any given time.

3) Use Split View for Efficiency: Split View is ideal when multitasking on your computer, opening two items side by side. For example, open a reference document and a writing app together to streamline your work.

4) Customize Your Spaces with Unique Wallpapers: Assign different wallpapers to spaces, making them visually different for letting your memory know which space is used for what.

5) Mission Control Shortcuts to Quickly Access: Master Mission Control shortcuts, such as using Control-Up Arrow and trackpad gestures, to see how much of a time-saver it is to access and organize your spaces.

CHAPTER 12: SYSTEM SETTINGS

To tailor your iMac experience, System Settings provides a central hub for modifying a wide range of options, from basic screen adjustments to accessibility features. Here's how you can navigate and modify these settings to personalize your iMac:

ACCESSING SYSTEM SETTINGS

1) Open System Settings: Start by clicking the System Settings icon directly in the Dock, or select it through the Apple menu at the top left of your screen, choosing (Apple Menu) > System Settings.

2) Navigating the Sidebar: The left sidebar contains a list of settings categories. Scroll down if needed to view all available options, and click on the specific setting you wish to change.

Choose the color
scheme for your Mac.

Click an item in the sidebar
to adjust settings.

MODIFYING KEY SETTINGS

1) Screen Saver and Wallpaper: Customize your display by choosing a screen saver, which you can also set as your wallpaper. This provides a cohesive visual experience and adds a personal touch to your desktop.

2) Notifications: Manage app alerts and notifications, tailoring which apps can send you alerts, when you'll receive them, and how they'll appear on your screen.

3) Display Settings: Adjust key display aspects, including brightness, color settings, and screen resolution, to enhance visibility and comfort based on your usage.

174

4) Accessibility: Fine-tune settings to make your iMac easier to use. Adjust features for vision, hearing, motor functions, and more to support a more inclusive experience.

KEEPING SOFTWARE UP TO DATE

In System Settings, you can also check for and install the latest macOS updates. Keeping your system updated ensures you have the newest features and important security patches.

FINDING SPECIFIC SETTINGS QUICKLY

If you're looking for a specific option but aren't sure where it's located, use the search bar at the top of the System Settings window. As you type, relevant settings will appear in the sidebar, allowing you to navigate directly to the option you need.

Each adjustment can significantly enhance your interaction with your iMac, making System Settings a versatile tool to ensure your Mac is optimized to suit your preferences.

LOCKING YOUR SCREEN

1) Setting Lock Screen Preferences: To secure your iMac when you're not actively using it, adjust the Lock Screen settings to automatically off the screen or activate a screen saver when a set period of inactivity elapses.

2) Enabling Password Requirements: For an additional layer of security, you can require a

password to open your screen when you get back. To set up these options:

a) Open System Settings.

b) Select Lock Screen from the sidebar.

c) From here, configure the idle time before the screen locks and activate the password requirement option to secure access.

CHOOSING AND CUSTOMIZING A SCREEN SAVER

1) Selecting a Screen Saver: Pick a screen saver which matches your style or mood by going to Screen Saver within System Settings. Apple offers a variety of screen savers, including Landscape, Cityscape, Earth, Underwater, and Shuffle Aerials themes.

2) Setting the Screen Saver as Wallpaper: If you'd like your screen saver to serve as your wallpaper, enable this option by turning on Show as Wallpaper in the Screen Saver settings. This transforms your display into a visually dynamic experience, even when you're not using your iMac.

CUSTOMIZING CONTROL CENTER AND MENU BAR

1) Choosing Control Center and Menu Bar Options: The Control Center on macOS gives you quick access to essential settings and frequently used tools. You can personalize the Control Center to fit your usage by selecting which settings appear

there, and even add shortcuts to the menu bar for easy access.
2) Adjusting Preferences: To customize:
   1. Go to System Settings.
   2. Click Control Center in the sidebar.
   3. From here, select the settings you want to include in the Control Center, and toggle the option to show them in the menu bar if desired.

UPDATING MACOS

1) Accessing Software Update: Regular updates ensure your iMac has the latest features, performance improvements, and security fixes. To check for updates:
   a) Open System Settings, then choose General from the sidebar.
   b) Click Software Update to see if a new version of macOS is available.
2) Enabling Automatic Updates: If you prefer automatic updates:
   a) In Software Update, toggle the "Automatically keep my Mac up to date" option.
   b) You can further specify whether you want macOS to automatically download updates, install system files, or include app updates from the App Store. This setup is highly beneficial to keep your iMac secure and up-to-date with minimal effort.

ICLOUD AND FAMILY SHARING SETTINGS

1) Signing into iCloud: iCloud syncs your files, photos, and app data across all your Apple devices, enhancing accessibility and convenience. To set up iCloud on your iMac:
   a) Open System Settings, click on your Apple ID at the sidebar's top, then select iCloud.
   b) Sign in using your Apple ID if you haven't already. Once signed in, you'll see a list of apps and services that can use iCloud.
2) Managing iCloud Storage and App Access:
   a) In the iCloud menu, review which apps and services are using iCloud storage and toggle off those you don't need synced.
   b) To manage your storage space, click Manage to view your iCloud usage and select options like Upgrade Storage if you need more space.
3) Managing Family Sharing: With Family Sharing, you can share your purchases, iCloud storage, and Apple subscriptions with family members.
   a) In System Settings, under Apple ID, select Family Sharing.
   b) Follow the prompts to invite family members using their Apple IDs. Once they accept, you can share iCloud storage, Apple Music, Apple TV+, and other services with them.
   c) You can also set up parental controls, manage Screen Time for each family member, even creating Apple ID for your child.

ADJUSTING TRUE TONE FOR AMBIENT LIGHT

1) Understanding True Tone: True Tone technology automatically adjusts the color temperature of your iMac's display based on the ambient lighting around you. This feature reduces the blue light from your screen in low-light environments and provides a more natural, eye-friendly viewing experience by adapting display warmth and coolness.
2) Turning True Tone On or Off:
   a) Open System Settings, then choose Displays from the sidebar.
   b) In the Displays section, toggle True Tone to enable or disable the feature based on your preference.
   c) When enabled, True Tone will seamlessly adjust display colors according to changes in ambient light, giving you the flexibility to work comfortably in different lighting conditions.

SETTING UP DYNAMIC DESKTOP FOR TIME-BASED VISUAL CHANGES

1) Using Dynamic Desktop: Dynamic Desktop is a feature that changes your wallpaper automatically to match the time of day, offering a visually engaging experience as the screen brightness and color tones adjust subtly throughout the day.
2) Selecting a Dynamic Desktop Wallpaper:
   a) Open System Settings, then choose Wallpaper from the sidebar.
   b) Scroll through the available wallpapers and select a Dynamic Desktop option, such as a

landscape or cityscape that will change from dawn to dusk.

3) Enabling Time-Based Changes:
   a) For the wallpaper to change automatically according to the time of day, Location Services should be turned on.
   b) If you've disabled Location Services, Dynamic Desktop will instead rely on the Date & Time settings, adjusting based on the time zone specified in your system.
   c) To enable Location Services, go to System Settings. Then click on **Privacy & Security** and choose **Location Services** and toggle it on.

CHANGING HOW ITEMS APPEAR ON THE SCREEN

1) Adjusting Display Resolution:
   a) To make items appear larger or smaller, you can modify the display resolution, which affects the size of everything on your screen, including windows, icons, and text.
   b) Go to System Settings and pick Displays from the sidebar.
   c) In the Displays settings, you'll see a section for Resolution. Choose Scaled to reveal available resolution options. Selecting a lower resolution makes items larger, while higher resolutions reduce item size for a sharper display.
2) Increasing Text and Icon Size:

a) For better readability, you can increase the size of icons and text without adjusting the full display resolution.
b) Go to System Settings and pick Accessibility > Display. Here, you can make text larger and increase icon size, improving ease of viewing without impacting the overall resolution.

3) Making the Pointer Easier to See:
a) You can adjust the appearance and visibility of the pointer to make it easier to find.
b) In System Settings, go to Accessibility > Display > Pointer. Adjust the pointer's size and color here. You can also enable the "Shake mouse pointer to locate" feature, which momentarily enlarges the pointer when you shake your mouse, making it easy to find on a cluttered screen.

ENABLING DARK MODE TO STAY FOCUSED

1) Activating Dark Mode:
a) Dark Mode provides a dark color scheme for your desktop, menu bar, Dock, and system apps, improving focus by making content stand out and reducing glare.
b) To enable Dark Mode, go to System Settings and pick Appearance from the sidebar.
c) In Appearance, choose Dark to activate Dark Mode across your iMac.

2) Optimizing for Dark Environments:

a) Dark Mode is especially useful for low-light environments, reducing eye strain and making it easier to view content without a bright screen.

b) When Dark Mode is enabled, system apps like Mail, Calendar, Contacts, and Messages display white text on a black background, which is easier to read in dark settings.

3) Benefits for Professional Image Editing:

a) Dark Mode is particularly beneficial for professionals working with images or videos, as it makes colors and fine details stand out against the darker background, offering better contrast.

b) Designers, photographers, and other creative professionals can maintain focus on their work, as Dark Mode allows them to better view colors and details with minimal distraction.

SETTING UP NIGHT SHIFT FOR WARMER COLORS

1) Understanding Night Shift: Night Shift reduces blue light by adjusting your screen to display warmer colors, which is beneficial at night or in low-light conditions. Research shows that blue light can interfere with sleep patterns, making it harder to wind down at the end of the day. Night Shift is designed to help you reduce exposure to blue light, encouraging a more restful evening.

2) Activating Night Shift:

a) Open System Settings and click Displays in the sidebar. At the bottom of the Displays settings, click Night Shift to access its options.
b) You have a few options for activating Night Shift:
   i) Manual Activation: Turn Night Shift on or off manually as needed.
   ii) Scheduled Activation: Schedule Night Shift to automatically switch on and off at times that suit your routine. You can specify a custom schedule or set it to activate automatically from sunset to sunrise, using your time zone to determine activation.
3) Adjusting the Color Temperature:
   a) In the Night Shift settings, you'll see a Color Temperature slider. This slider allows you to fine-tune the warmth of your screen colors when Night Shift is active.
   b) Dragging the slider towards Less Warm will keep more blue light, while moving it towards More Warm will reduce blue light further, creating a warmer screen appearance.
   c) Test different levels of warmth to see which setting is most comfortable, especially in low-light or night time environments.

CONNECTING AN EXTERNAL DISPLAY

1) Determining Display Support:
   a) Before connecting an external display, projector, or HDTV, check how many external displays your iMac supports. This can vary

depending on the specific model and hardware capabilities.

   b) To check this, go to System Settings and pick Help > iMac Specifications from the menu. In the specifications, locate the Video Support section, where the number of supported external displays will be listed. You may need to scroll to find this section.

2) Connecting Your External Display:

   a) Your iMac should have one or more Thunderbolt or HDMI ports for connecting external displays. Ensure you have the appropriate cable and, if necessary, an adapter.

   b) Connect the external display to the port on your iMac. Your iMac should automatically detect the new display and mirror or extend your screen based on your existing settings.

3) Configuring Display Settings:

   a) Once connected, Open System Settings, then choose Displays to configure how your iMac interacts with the external display.

   b) You can choose to Mirror Displays if you want the same content to appear on both screens, or Use as Separate Display to extend your desktop and have additional screen space for multitasking.

   c) In the Displays settings, you'll also have the choice of setting the resolution and orientation for each connected display, allowing you to customize each one according to your needs.

CHAPTER 13: SETTING UP AND ENABLING SCREEN TIME

Activating Screen Time:

1) To start, Open System Settings, then choose Screen Time from the sidebar. If you haven't enabled it yet, you'll need to turn it on.

2) Screen Time will begin tracking usage from the time it's enabled, gathering data on app and website usage, notifications, and how often the device is picked up. Once on, you can dive into a variety of detailed reports and options.

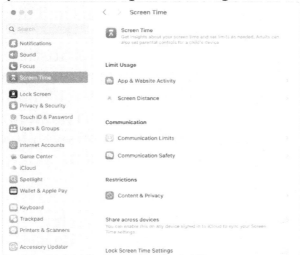

VIEWING HOW YOU USE YOUR IMAC

1) App & Website Activity:
   a) The App & Website Activity report shows how much time you're spending on individual apps and websites each day and week. This can help

you understand where most of your time goes and identify potentially excessive usage patterns.

b) In System Settings, under Screen Time, click App & Website Activity to access these statistics. From here, you'll see an organized list of apps and websites ranked by usage time, allowing for an in-depth look at your digital habits.

2) Notifications Report:

a) The Notifications report helps you see which apps send the most notifications, which can give insight into interruptions and distractions during your day.

b) To view notifications statistics, select Notifications in the Screen Time menu. Apps will be listed by the number of notifications they've sent, making it easy to pinpoint sources of distraction. This data allows you to consider limiting certain notifications for a more focused experience.

3) Pickups:

a) The Pickups report reveals how often you actively engage with your device, such as opening the screen or starting new sessions. Frequent pickups may indicate a habit of checking the device frequently, even when it may not be necessary.

b) To view this information, click Pickups in the Screen Time settings. Here, you'll see data on the frequency of pickups and the time intervals in which they occur.

SETTING DOWNTIME AND APP LIMITS

1) Downtime:
   a) Downtime is a feature designed to help you step away from the screen, especially during certain hours, by restricting access to specified apps. While in downtime, just those applications which you chose to allow (such as phone calls or essential work apps) will be accessible.
   b) To set up Downtime, go to Screen Time in System Settings and pick Downtime. Choose a schedule for when downtime should be active, such as daily during evening hours. Customizing this schedule helps encourage breaks and healthy device usage.
2) App Limits:
   a) App Limits lets you set time limits for specific apps or app categories, such as social media or entertainment, helping to control usage by capping the time spent in these areas.
   b) In System Settings under Screen Time, select App Limits. Click Add Limit and pick the applications or categories which you'll like to restrict. You can set different time limits for each day or a daily limit across all days, depending on your goals.

USING SCREEN TIME FOR FAMILY SHARING

1) Monitor Family Members' Usage:
   a) If you have parental privileges in a Family Sharing group, you can use Screen Time to monitor and manage how much time each family member, especially children, spends on their devices. This includes setting App Limits and Downtime remotely.
   b) In System Settings, go to Screen Time and select the family member's name from the sidebar. Here, you'll be able to view their usage reports, set limits, and customize controls as needed.

2) Requesting More Time:
   a) Family members with set limits can request additional time when they reach a limit. This feature is particularly useful for parents, as it allows children to request more screen time only when they need it.
   b) Parents receive notifications for time requests, allowing them to approve or deny additional time based on each situation.

SETTING LIMITS FOR YOURSELF

1) Access Screen Time: Begin by opening Your iMac's System Settings. In the sidebar, locate and select Screen Time to access the various settings available for monitoring and controlling your device usage.

2) Activating Downtime:
   a) To set limits on your usage, you will first want to configure Downtime. Downtime allows you to schedule periods during which only selected apps can be accessed, effectively limiting distractions during specific hours.
   b) Click on Downtime in the Screen Time menu. Toggle the switch to On to activate this feature.
3) Creating a Schedule:
   a) Once Downtime is activated, you will need to establish a schedule. Click on the Schedule pop-up menu to choose between a daily schedule or a custom one for each day of the week.
   b) For a daily schedule, simply select the time frame during which you want Downtime to be active. For instance, if you prefer to disconnect in the evenings, you might set Downtime from 9 PM to 7 AM.
   c) For custom schedules, select each day of the week and assign different time frames as needed. This flexibility allows you to tailor your downtime based on varying commitments throughout the week.
4) App Limits for Specific Apps:
   a) To further refine how you manage your app usage, consider setting app limits for individual apps or categories of apps. This feature is particularly beneficial for controlling time spent on social media, gaming, or entertainment apps.

b) In the Screen Time menu, click on App Limits. Then, click Add Limit to choose from a list of app categories or select specific apps you wish to limit.

c) After selecting the apps or categories, set a time limit for daily usage. You can modify limits for various days if necessary, giving you complete control over how much time you will spend on particular apps.

ENSURING YOU DON'T MISS IMPORTANT THINGS

1) Configuring Always Allowed Apps:
   a) While Downtime restricts app access, there may be certain applications or websites you want to ensure are always accessible, such as communication tools or essential work applications.
   b) In the menu for Screen Time, choose Always Allowed. Inside, you can manage which apps remain available during your Downtime hours.

2) Enabling Always Allowed Apps:
   a) A list of apps will appear, and you can toggle on the ones you want to keep available. For example, you might want to keep Messages, FaceTime, or any other important productivity tools active.
   b) Make sure to select apps that you need immediate access to for urgent communications or essential tasks, allowing

you to stay connected without entirely sacrificing your Downtime intentions.

3) Managing Website Access:

a) In addition to apps, you can also specify websites that should remain accessible. Under the Always Allowed section, click on the option to manage website access. This could be beneficial for allowing access to educational or work-related websites during Downtime.

b) Ensure you regularly review and adjust these settings as needed, particularly if your schedule changes or your priorities shift.

CHAPTER 14: SETTINGS SCREEN TIME FOR YOUR CHILD

Setting up Screen Time for a child on your iMac can help you manage their digital habits and ensure they have a safe and balanced experience online. There are two primary methods for doing this: using Family Sharing for remote management or setting up Screen Time directly on your child's Mac account. Here's a detailed, step-by-step guide for each approach.

STEP 1: ACCESS SYSTEM SETTINGS

2) Open System Settings:

  a) Click on the Apple menu (🍎) located in the upper-left corner of your screen.
  b) Pick System Settings from the dropdown menu. This will open the System Settings window where you can adjust various settings for your Mac.

3) Locate Screen Time:

  a) In the System Settings sidebar, scroll down until you find Screen Time ⏳. Click on it to access the Screen Time settings.

STEP 2: CHOOSE YOUR CHILD

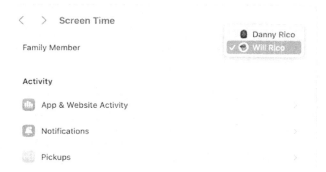

1) Once in the Screen Time settings, look for the pop-up menu for the Family Member. This menu allows you to select which family member's Screen Time settings you want to adjust.

2) Click on the pop-up menu and choose your child's name from the list of family members. If you do not see the pop-up menu for the Family Member, ensure that you are signed into your Apple Account and that you're using Family Sharing.

STEP 3: SETTING UP SCREEN TIME FOR A CHILD

1) Turn On Screen Time:
   a) After selecting your child, click on **Set Up Screen Time For Your Child**.
   b) A new window will appear prompting you to Turn on Screen Time. Click the button to activate this feature.

2) Follow Onscreen Instructions: The setup process will guide you through several options:
   a) Content Restrictions: You can set restrictions on certain types of content based on age ratings

for movies, TV shows, apps, and websites. This helps ensure your child has access only to age-appropriate content.

b) Screen Distance: This feature reminds your child to maintain a safe distance from the screen, which can help reduce eye strain.

c) App & Website Activity: Enable this to monitor which apps and websites your child is using most frequently.

d) Time Away from Screens: You can set specific time periods when your child should be away from screens, promoting healthy breaks and balanced usage.

e) Screen Time Passcode: Create a four-digit passcode that will be required to access Screen Time settings and to approve additional screen time when limits are reached. This ensures that your child cannot alter the settings without your permission.

STEP 4: CONFIGURE SCREEN TIME OPTIONS

1) Include Website Data:
    a) Scroll down in the Screen Time settings and look for the Include Website Data option.
    b) Turn on this option if you want Screen Time reports to provide detailed information about specific websites visited by your child. Without this enabled, usage will be reported only as general Safari usage, limiting your ability to monitor web activity effectively.

2) Lock Screen Time Settings:
   a) Look for the Lock Screen Time Settings option.
   b) Turn this option on to require the Screen Time passcode whenever someone attempts to access the Screen Time settings. This prevents unauthorized changes and allows you to maintain control over the limits you've set.
   c) If your child has an administrator account, You are going to be prompted to convert it to a standard account. This ensures that the Screen Time settings can be enforced effectively without the ability to override them.

STEP 5: REVIEW OTHER SCREEN TIME FEATURES AND SETTINGS

Having set up Screen Time, there are quite several other features you may want to implement to give this feature a nice wrap. Each of these options is discussed in some detail below:

1. APP & WEBSITE ACTIVITY

View Usage Reports:
1) Click on App & Website Activity within the Screen Time settings. Here, you can see detailed reports about how much time your child spends on different apps and websites.
2) The reports display the amount of time spent on each app, the frequency of app usage, and which websites were accessed. This information helps

you understand your child's habits and make informed decisions about screen time limits.

3) Notification Insights: This section also includes details about which apps send the most notifications. By monitoring these notifications, you can help reduce distractions and encourage healthier usage patterns.

2. DOWNTIME

Scheduling Breaks:

1) Click on Downtime to set specific periods during which your child will be unable to use most apps and features on their device.

2) You can choose a daily schedule or customize different times for each day of the week. For example, you might set downtime from 8 PM to 7 AM on school nights to ensure your child is getting enough rest.

3) During this period, only apps that you've designated as Always Allowed will be accessible. This helps to ensure that important apps like Phone or Messages remain available while still limiting overall screen time.

3. APP LIMITS

Setting Time Limits:

1) Click on App Limits to create specific time restrictions for single apps or categories of apps (like Social Networking or Games).

2) You can set daily limits that will apply to the selected apps, and once the limit is reached, the apps will be blocked for the remainder of the day.
3) This feature encourages your child to be mindful of their usage, helping them develop better habits regarding how much time they spend on different activities.

4. ALWAYS ALLOWED

Essential Apps:
1) Click on Always Allowed to select apps that your child can use at any time, even during Downtime.
2) For instance, you might want to ensure that apps like Messages, Phone, or specific educational tools are always available to them. This is especially useful for maintaining open lines of communication or for educational purposes without completely sacrificing limits on entertainment apps.

5. SCREEN DISTANCE

Health Alerts:
1) Click on Screen Distance to enable alerts that remind your child to maintain a proper distance from the screen. This is important for eye health, particularly for younger users.
2) When the device detects that it's being held too close to the face, a notification will prompt your child to adjust the distance. This feature encourages good habits that can help prevent eye strain.

6. COMMUNICATION LIMITS

Setting Communication Boundaries:
1) Click on Communication Limits to define who your child can communicate with through Messages and FaceTime.
2) You can set limits on communication during screen time and downtime, allowing you to control who can reach out to your child during specific periods. This is a critical feature for ensuring your child's safety in online interactions.

7. COMMUNICATION SAFETY

Sensitive Photo Checks:
1) Click on Communication Safety to enable features that check for sensitive photos in messages sent or received by your child.
2) If inappropriate or explicit content is detected, the feature can alert you and provide your child with warnings, ensuring they are not exposed to harmful material.

8. CONTENT & PRIVACY

Restricting Access:
1) Click on Content & Privacy to set restrictions on explicit content, purchases, downloads, as well as privacy settings.
2) You can block access to adult websites, limit the use of specific apps, and manage what types of content can be viewed in the iTunes and App Store.

3) Additionally, you can set privacy settings that restrict your child's ability to change settings or access certain features without your permission, providing peace of mind about their online interactions and usage.

SETTING UP SCREEN TIME WITHOUT FAMILY SHARING

If you prefer not to utilize Family Sharing, you still have the option to set up Screen Time directly on your child's Mac account:

1) Log into Your Child's Account: Switch to your child's user account on their iMac. If they do not have an account yet, create one through System Settings under Users & Groups.

2) Access Screen Time: Open System Settings while logged into your child's account and locate Screen Time in the sidebar.

3) Activate Screen Time: Toggle Screen Time to On. You'll be prompted to create a passcode to prevent your child from changing these settings.

4) Customize Settings: Just like in the Family Sharing method, set up Downtime, App Limits, and Always Allowed apps based on your preferences for their usage. Additionally, activate Content & Privacy Restrictions to block inappropriate content and manage app access.

5) Regular Check-Ins: Make it a habit to regularly check in on your child's Screen Time reports to monitor their activity and ensure that the limits

set are appropriate for their age and responsibilities.

FINAL CONSIDERATIONS

1) Regular Monitoring: Once Screen Time is set up, regularly check in on your child's usage reports. This will help you understand their habits and adjust the settings as necessary.
2) Communication: Discuss with your child why these limits are in place. Engaging them in the conversation can foster understanding and cooperation.
3) Default Settings for Under-13 kids: For children under 13, certain features like Screen Distance & Communication Safety are automatically enabled. The Web Content Filter will block adult content, providing an additional layer of security.
4) Adaptability: As your child grows and their needs change, revisit and adjust these settings to ensure they align with their maturity level and activities.

MANAGING DOWNTIME

Managing Downtime in Screen Time on your iMac is an essential step towards fostering healthy screen habits for both you and your children. Here's a comprehensive guide to managing downtime effectively:

UNDERSTANDING DOWNTIME IN SCREEN TIME

Downtime is a feature within Screen Time that allows you to designate specific periods during which you or your children cannot use most apps or features on the Mac. During this time, only the apps you've designated as Always Allowed can be accessed. Downtime helps you balance technology use with other important activities, encouraging breaks and healthier habits. This is especially useful for encouraging family time, study periods, or restful nights.

DOWNTIME SETUP

1) Enable Screen Time
   a) For you to be able to set up Downtime, you have to enable Screen Time. Go to the Apple Menu and then pick System Settings > Screen Time and click on the Turn On Screen Time.
   b) If setting for a child, make sure to choose their account under the pop-up menu for the Family Member.
2) Access Downtime Settings: From within Screen Time settings, select Downtime in the sidebar. You may set here times when Downtime should be on.

SETTING A SCHEDULE FOR DOWNTIME STEP BY STEP

Step 1: Enter Screen Time Settings

1) Launch System Settings: Click the Apple menu at the very top of your screen. Select System Setting from drop down menu
2) Proceed to Screen Time: In the System Settings window, Screen Time should be available in the sidebar; if you can't see it immediately, scroll down.

Step 2: Select Family Member
1) If you are a parent or guardian managing a child's account through Family Sharing, click the pop-up menu for the Family Member. It lets you select for which family member you want to change the Downtime settings.
2) If you are not seeing the pop-up menu for the Family Member, then sign in again for Apple Account; make sure Family Sharing settings are appropriate.

Step 3: Go to Downtime Settings:
1) Once you selected the correct family member-or yourself- Downtime option in the Screen Time settings.
2) If you do not see the Downtime option, it simply means that you have not enabled Screen Time for the family member you have selected. You will need to enable Screen Time first.

Step 4: Set Up Your Downtime Schedule

Click on Downtime. This is going to reveal the Downtime settings options.

Schedule Options:
1) Set a Standard Schedule:
   a) If you want the same hours of Downtime each day, click the Schedule pop-up menu, then choose Every Day.
   b) Choose the start and end times for Downtime. For example, you might choose 8 PM to 7 AM so as not to disturb sleeping downtown for evening activities.

2) Set Custom Daily Schedules:
   a) To have different hours of Downtime for different days, select Custom from the Schedule menu.
   b) Toggle on or off which days of the week you'll like to enable Downtime for, selecting start and end times: for example,
      i) 8 PM - 7 AM, Monday - Friday
      ii) 10 PM - 9 AM, Saturday
      iii)9 PM - 8 AM, Sunday

This enables you to have different routines at various times of the week.

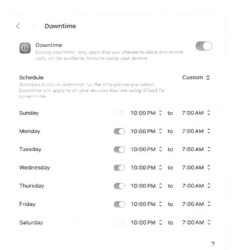

Step 5: Block Device Access During Downtime

1) You can turn on Block at Downtime if you need to completely shut off access to the device when in Downtime. This option only appears if you have ever set a Screen Time passcode.

2) **What is Blocking?** When On it completely blocks the user from accessing Mac completely during the scheduled hours of Downtime. This actually enforces what is meant by taking a break from screen time.

BEST PRACTICES FOR SETTING UP DOWNTIME

1) Talk to Family Members: When you impose Downtime, especially on your children, talk about why limits to screen time are important, and the benefits from this action. You have to explain to

them the fact that Downtime encourages other activities like reading and spending time with the family or practicing hobbies.

2) Adjust as Needed: Follow the effectiveness of your Downtime schedule over time. If your routine of the family changes, then you should not give a second thought to changing the start and end times to better fit everyone's needs.

3) Use Always Allowed Apps Wisely: During the setting up of Downtime, you are able to specify which apps must remain accessible at all times, even during Downtime-this is essential for any highly important communication or educational apps.

   a) Under Screen Time settings, tap on Always Allowed to select those apps that you want to always keep available, such as Messages, Phone, or some other tool related to education.

   b) Now, you have to think about which apps need to be available during Downtime. Mark the apps that hold importance in your life for communication and education, like Messages, Notes, or anything relating to education, as Always Allowed to keep the important functionalities running.

4) Daily Usage Reports: Review daily usage reports on how effective Downtime is through the App & Website Activity-which can give you an insight into how much screen time is being logged, and when adjustments in the schedule should be made for Downtime.

5) Encouraging Healthy Habits:
   a) It is not just a matter of setting a limit on screen time using Downtime, but also to help build healthier routines and habits in general. Encourage reading, family games, or outdoor activities during Downtime.
   b) Let your children understand that this is necessary for them to have breaks and why they must limit the amount of screen time. This way, they will appreciate the importance of Downtime rather than it being a punishment.

STEP-BY-STEPS GUIDE FOR TURNING DOWNTIME SCHEDULE ON OR OFF

1) Open Screen Time Settings:
   a) Click Apple menu icon within your top left corner of your screen.
   b) Pick System Settings from the dropdown menu. This opens the main settings interface for your Mac.
   c) Scroll down the sidebar in the System Settings window and click on Screen Time.

6) Select Family Member-if Applicable
   a) Select the pop-up menu for the Family Member if you set up Family Sharing to manage Downtime for a child or another family member.
   b) Select the family member for which you want to enable or disable the Downtime schedule. This is really helpful for parents who need to

manage and control their kids' device use. To do this,

c) If the pop-up menu for the Family Member isn't available, ensure you have signed in with your Apple Account and that Family Sharing is appropriately set.

4. Open Downtime Settings: Once the right family member (which could be you yourself) is selected, the **Downtime** option can be found in Screen Time settings. Tap to reveal all Downtime configuration options.

5. **Change the Downtime Schedule**

a) Using Schedule Pop-up Menu: There will be a Schedule pop-up menu from where the status of your Downtime settings can be changed.

b) Turn On the Downtime Schedule: To turn on Downtime, tap Schedule and then select from:

i) Every Day: If you chose this, you need to enter in all your start and end times for Downtime. This is the best if you have a fixed time you want Downtime on, such as from 8 PM to 7 AM, throughout a week.

ii) Custom: Through this, you can specify a different Downtime for every day of the week. You may want this in cases where you want different hours for your weekends compared to weekdays. You will need to specify the start and end time on each day for this type.

2) To Turn Off the Downtime Schedule:

a) To have the Downtime schedule off click, **Off** from the Schedule pop-up menu.

b) ·To turn off the schedule simply means that Downtime restrictions will not be applied until you choose to turn it back on. You can at any time go back to that same schedule later by easily following the steps and selecting previous settings.

BEST PRACTICES FOR MANAGING DOWNTIME

1) Consider Your Reasons for Downtime: Regularly review the current Downtime schedule: whether it is working for you or if you need to make some adjustments. Be flexible: some weeks you may want to manage more or less screen time.

2) Talk About Changes: What to say: If you are changing the Downtime schedule for kids, be open. Explain why the schedule is off or different and encourage talking about healthy ways to use screens.

3) Purposeful Use of Downtime: Add Downtime not just to reduce screen time, but to encourage other activities. Use this window of time to unite the family, read, or head outdoors.

4) Stay engaged with your Screen Time Reports: Regularly review app usage and screen time reports so changes to a child's Downtime schedule support the bigger reasons for device use in your family.

CONTENT AND PRIVACY RESTRICTIONS

Setting up Content & Privacy Restrictions on your iMac is one great thing to control and limit types of access to different content, apps, and features. This will, in particular, be very helpful if you're a parent, guardian, or any other person who wants more rigid restrictions on the content available to someone using your Mac. This applies across applications, web content, in-app purchases, Siri & Game Center, among many others. We will now walk you through the step-by-step process of how to turn on these settings in Screen Time on Mac.

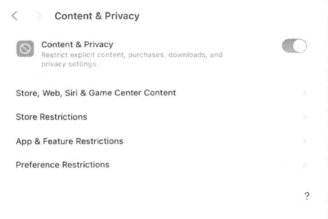

PRE-REQUISITES FOR SETTING CONTENT & PRIVACY RESTRICTIONS

Before you can proceed to setting up the content and privacy restrictions, Screen Time must have first been activated. This is because Screen Time keeps track of device usage and applies the restriction. To enable Screen Time:

1) Go to Apple menu and then pick System Settings.

2) Tap Screen Time from the sidebar; toggle the switch if not already on.

CONFIGURATION OF CONTENT AND PRIVACY RESTRICTIONS IN STEP-BY-STEP MANNER

STEP 1: OPEN SCREEN TIME SETTINGS

1) System Settings: If an iMac is used, click on the upper left side Apple menu and select System Settings.
2) Scroll down and click on Screen Time in the sidebar.

STEP 2: LOCATE THE FAMILY MEMBER

1) Locate Family Member (if required): Select Family Member from the pop-up menu, if you are part of a Family Sharing group and you want to set up restrictions for a child or another family member.
2) Select the family member on which you'd like to use the content and privacy restrictions. If you can't see Family Member, sign in with your Apple Account and check you have set up Family Sharing correctly.

STEP 3: TURN CONTENT & PRIVACY ON

1) Content & Privacy On: With the family member selected, locate and tap the Content & Privacy option in the Screen Time settings.
2) If it is toggled off, click on the toggle beside this feature to turn it on.

STEP 4: LIMITING CONTENT AND ACTIVITIES

With Content & Privacy turned on, you'll see several categories of restrictions. It also allows different kinds of controls that block access to certain content, actions, and features of iPad. Example:

1) Content from App Store, the Web, Siri & the Game Center: This will let you control what kind of web content is accessible and limit in-app features.
2) You can turn on and off such options restricting access to specific categories of websites, restricting Siri's web search, and Game Center content based on age appropriateness.
3) Web restrictions may include an option between blocking adult content and limiting browsing to previously approved websites only

STEP 5: PUT RESTRICTIONS ON STORE PURCHASING AND MEDIA

1) Click **Store Restrictions** to begin enabling the capability to restrict access to purchasing options within the Apple Store.
2) Here, you can restrict the film, television, and app types that can be bought or downloaded. In addition, some of these limitations prevent unintended in-app purchasing with age-restricted content.
3) The Store Restrictions are quite helpful to the parents in managing the type of media your children can access and buy on their devices.

STEP 6: LIMIT APPS AND FEATURES

1) Click **App & Feature Restrictions** to specify which apps and features should be available. This functionality extends to control availability of apps based on their content-for instance, social networking, games, or productivity applications.

2) Enabling these options does not allow unauthorized changes in the Mac's configurations. This comes in handy if you have children or others that are frequently using this device.

3) For example, you can exercise the changes within the password settings, internet account sharing setting option to offer greater control over the system stability and security.

BENEFITS AND BEST PRACTICES

The Setting Content & Privacy Restrictions offer more control over device use and help in building a much safer digital environment. Here are a few tips about how you can leverage such settings best:

1) Customize Restrictions for Age: Most children use devices across many years of development. If you set up restrictions for your child, tailor it according to age and maturity. Younger children may benefit from broader restrictions, while teens might need more flexibility with oversight.

2) Periodic Report Reviewing: Check Screen Time reports for App & Website Activity on how the Mac is being used to give an insight into what one wants to change concerning restriction settings.

In this manner, you will be provided with opportunities to make informed choices.

3) Balance Restrictions and Access: Be sure not to make the restrictions over-constraining regarding essential educational or productivity apps. It is in the balancing that safe use without hindrance of access to helpful resources is realized.

4) Tailoring to Individual Family Members: With Family Sharing, you can establish restrictions for each child differently, or on each member of the family. To do this, tap the pop-up menu for the Family Member to select family members and establish special content and privacy controls as needed.

CONCLUSION

Setting up Content and Privacy Restrictions on your iMac amounts to a powerful toolset that one can use to restrict the kind of content and features accessible on the device. This feature is very important for families in that it can help parents create a much safer and more age-appropriate digital environment for their children.

CHAPTER 15: MANAGING WINDOWS

Window management on iMacs is key to keeping your workspace clean and organized, especially when working with a lot of applications that may require several windows open simultaneously. Here are the major tools and techniques in macOS that make window organization efficient:

PREVIEW

FULL-SCREEN MODE FOR FOCUS ON A SINGLE APP

Full-Screen Mode lets an app take over the entire screen to help minimize distractions from other open apps and lets you focus on a closer view of your work. This is beneficial for projects that are very immersive, such as writing, video editing, or graphics design.

How to Enter Full Screen Mode

1) Open an application you wish to use in full screen mode.
2) Tap the green button with two arrows in any application window's top left corner or hover your mouse over it and select Enter Full Screen.
3) The application now fills your entire display while other applications disappear from view until you return to this view.

Exiting Full Screen Mode

Take your mouse over to the screen's top to see the menu bar, and then tap the green button again, or hit Control + Command + F.

SPLIT VIEW FOR MULTI-TASKING WITH TWO APPS

Split View ideal when you want to work with two apps right beside each other, like referencing a document you have typed while taking notes, or having the web open beside a video.

How to Use Split View

1) Open the first application, hover your cursor over the green full-screen button and select either Tile Window to Left of Screen or Tile Window to Right of Screen.
2) Open the second app and it will automatically fill in the screen's adjacent side.

Adjusting the Split

To resize the split, drag the vertical line between the two windows to give one app more space.

Exiting Split View

Click to close one of the apps or click the green button to exit full-screen mode; either will collapse Split View and return both apps to their separate windows.

STAGE MANAGER FOR AUTOMATIC WINDOW MANAGEMENT

Stage Manager is an option for auto-arrangement of open apps on your desktop. Because windows are grouped together by default, Stage Manager reduces desktop clutter and makes it easy to switch between groups.

How to Activate Stage Manager

1) Click the Apple Menu and then pick System Settings.
2) Click the Desktop & Dock inside the sidebar.
3) Put on Stage Manager to have your desktop automatically organized.

Using Stage Manager

1) Active App: The active app window is brought in sharp focus in the center of your screen.
2) Grouped Windows: Other open apps or windows are minimized onto the left sidebar. You can click these to bring them up to the foreground.
3) App Switching: Click any app in the sidebar to bring that into the main view, replacing the current app. This setup is perfect for users who want a number of different apps open but have a streamlined way of toggling between them without cluttering the main workspace.

MISSION CONTROL FOR QUICK ACCESS TO ALL OPEN WINDOWS

Mission Control unleashes a layer that shows you all of your open windows, desktops, and full-screen apps in an organized overview, so you can look at everything running on your Mac in one instant. And it is quite helpful when you need to find that one window or app buried underneath all others.

How to Open Mission Control

1) Scroll up with three fingers on your trackpad, or press your keyboard's F3 key (Mission Control key).
2) All open windows will appear in a tiled view as well as other open spaces and full-screen applications will appear at the top.

Using Mission Control

1) To bring any window to the foreground, click on it
2) To add a new desktop space hover over the top then click the "+" button on top.

MULTIPLE DESKTOP SPACES (VIRTUAL DESKTOPS)

Multiple desktop spaces, called "Spaces," let you set up virtual desktops for various activities or projects you're working on and then easily switch between them. For example, you can have one space with work applications open and another space with personal things.

Creation and Spaces Switching

1) Open Mission Control described above.
2) In the top bar, click the "+" sign to add a new desktop.

3) To switch between spaces, three-finger swipe on your trackpad left or right or use Control + Left/Right Arrow

Moving Windows Between Spaces

Drag one window from one space to the other at the top of the screen in Mission Control

Multiple spaces are very good to split your work depending on different projects or workflows; you are going to be able to keep all of your stuff organized and jump between contexts really fast.

USING FULL-SCREEN VIEW ON IMAC

Full-Screen View opens one application window to fill the entire display screen, so that you don't see any other applications, the Dock, or the menu bar; you work only with the active application.

How to Enter Full-Screen View

1) Open the application you want to work in.
2) Click the green button at the top-left side of your application window; it contains two arrows.
3) Hover the green button, and from its drop-down menu select Full Screen - or simply click on the button.

When you go into full screen, your whole screen will be accommodated by the app, covering everything else running and background distractions.

How To access the Menu Bar and the Dock which are Hidden:

1) Menu Bar: Just take your pointer to the top of the screen; the menu bar will reappear.
2) Dock: In case your dock is automatically hidden, you only have to move your pointer towards the bottom of the screen. You can also set your preference to not auto-hide the dock in System Settings > Desktop & Dock.

How to Quit Full-Screen Mode
1) Viewing green button, move cursor at the top of the screen.
2) Green button - Click to Quit full-screen mode OR press Control + Command + F.

Always Show Menu Bar:
You can change settings to let the menu bar appear during full-screen mode. To do so, follow these steps:
1) Open the Apple menu, click System Settings, and proceed to click Desktop & Dock.
2) Turn off the option to *make the menu bar disappear and reappear when you go full screen* so that it remains always visible at times when in full screen for easy access to tools.

USING SPLIT VIEW ON IMAC

With Split View, you can work with two app windows side by side, each taking half of the screen. This really comes in handy with those working projects when you need to refer to information from one app while working in another-appropriate for such tasks like researching and writing, or comparing documents side by side.

Click to see
window options.

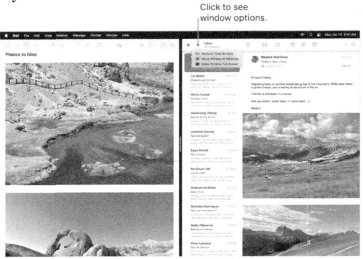

How to Turn On Split View:

1) Open the first app window that you want to set up with Split View.

2) Once the app window is active, to move the tile window to the left or right side of the screen, place your mouse pointer over the green button located in the window's upper left corner and select the desired option.

3) The window will jump to the half of the screen you chose while other currently open apps are listed as choices for the opposite half.

4) Click the other app window you want on the opposite side of the screen, and it will automatically fill the remaining half of the screen.

Once in Split View, each app occupies one-half of the screen, and you can work in both windows without having to manually resize them.

Resizing Windows in Split View:

1) A vertical bar divides two·app windows when in Split View.

2) Drag this bar to set the relative amount of screen space given to each app. This is helpful if one application requires more focus than another.

App Switching and Quitting Split View:

1) In order to replace one of the applications in Split View, hover over the green button; other options will come up, and you can replace the application in one half of your screen.

2) To exit Split View, click the green button of one of your app windows, or press Esc. Both windows will return to their normal size.

Full-Screen Mode of Each App in Split View:

If you want to focus on one app from the Split View, you can go full screen by positioning your cursor at the screen's top and choosing Full Screen from among the options given through the green button.

FULL SCREEN VS SPLIT VIEW:

1) Full: Good for focusing on a single app without distractions

2) Split: Good for multitasking in general: using two apps side-by-side without clutter of more windows

TILING WINDOWS ON IMAC

221

The tiling of windows allows you to organize your applications on the screen without any overlap and hence easily see several documents or programs all at once. Here is how it is done.

How to Tile Windows

1. Open Application: Open all applications or windows that you want to tile on your iMac.
2. Locate Green Button: The green button is located near the top-left of the window. It consists of two arrows pulling in opposite directions. This is the same button used to make things full-screen and now is used for tiling.
3. Enable Tiling: Bring your pointer over the green button. The drop-down opens showing options for tiling. Select Your Arrangement:
4. Tile Window to Left of Screen: This will move the selected window to the left half of your screen.
5. Tile Window to Right of Screen: This will position the window on the right half of the screen.
6. Once one of these is selected, the window will snap to that side of the screen.
7. Click on the Second Window: After having one window tiled, the rest of the open windows will show upon the other half of the screen. Click the window that you want to occupy another half of the screen, and it will automatically fill that half of the screen.

Resizing Tiled Windows :

1. Window Resizing: By dragging the dividing vertical line separating the two windows in tiles,

you will be able to resize windows. This will give more screen space to the application that you are working on.

2. Tiled Apps Switching: In order to switch the running application in one of the positions, just hovering over the green button of another window you want to switch to and clicking on the tiling option again will do the deal.

MORE WINDOW MANAGEMENT TIPS

Clean Up Your Desktop in a Jiffy:

On occasions, opening a lot of windows could crowd your desktop. You might want to work or open some files on the desktop, so follow these steps when it comes to clearing the view, easily and at once:

1) Click on the Desktop Wallpaper: Press anywhere on your desktop wallpaper. This automatically minimizes all the windows that have been opened up and you can clearly see the desktop itself.

2) Reopen Your Windows: To restore your windows, click on the desktop wallpaper again. All the previously minimized windows will appear to the last position, and you can easily carry on with your work.

Managing your Windows with Mission Control:

1) Mission Control: It is another useful feature that allows the user to view all the currently open

windows along with open spaces all at once. To use Mission Control:

a) Swipe three or four fingers up on your trackpad or press the F3 key-or at least the key with three rectangles on the top row of your keyboard.

b) It provides an overview of all applications opened and their windows to select the one you want more easily.

USING SPLIT VIEW FOR EXTEND

While tiling windows is great for side-by-side viewing, try Split View to take multitasking to the next level below:

How to Turn on Split View:

1) Tile one window using the previous steps

2) Select a second window to open to fill the remaining part of the screen.

3) Split View allows both applications to be viewed and engaged without overlap.

WIDGETS ON YOUR IMAC DESKTOP

Widgets are small applications that let you access information or perform day-to-day tasks quickly and all from your desktop without consuming too much space. Here's how to add, remove, and rearrange widgets:

1) Managing Your Widgets: To do this, click the time and date in your menu bar at the top of the screen. This opens the Notification Center.

2) Alternatively, right-click anywhere on the desktop background and click Edit Widgets from the context menu.

3) Adding Widgets: With the widget gallery now opened, you will see different varieties of widgets available. These may include events in your calendar, weather information, reminders, and others. Browse through the available widgets. Each widget may offer different sizes or options to display specific information.

4) To add a widget, simply drag it from the gallery to your desktop or Notification Center. You can place it anywhere you like, customizing your layout based on your preference.

5) Removing Widgets:
   a) To remove a widget from your desktop, hover over the widget until you see the remove button appear-usually a small "x" or a minus sign.

b) Use the remove button to delete the widget from your desktop.
6) Rearranging Widgets:
   a) You can reorder widgets by clicking and dragging them where you'd like, so you can work in a layout that best suits your workflow.
   b) To resize some widgets, you may find options either in the widget gallery or on the widget itself for showing small, medium, or large sizes.
7) Adding iPhone Widgets: If you are signed into one Apple ID on both your iOS device and Mac, then you can directly add the widgets from your iPhone to the Mac desktop. This serves well for continuity whereby you will have access to your favorite iPhone widgets without having to install corresponding apps into your Mac.
8) Customization Of Widgets: Once you have set up your widgets, it's often possible to personalize their look - theme or data to display, for example - by clicking on the widget itself and delving into its settings. This feature lets you personalise the information within the widget for better optimisation of it.

STAGE MANAGER

Essentially, Stage Manager is a feature designed to keep tidiness on your desktop. It does this by putting your opened apps and windows in order automatically, keeping clutter minimal but still keeping your active tasks at hand. In this tutorial, we're going to give you a run for your money, showing how to work effectively with Stage Manager. Here's how to utilize Stage Manager:

Enable Stage Manager
1) Open the Control Center: Begin by tapping the Control Center icon in your menu bar; it has the icon of two switches. This opens a group of options for the management of system settings.
2) Then enable Stage Manager: Find Stage Manager in Control Center and tap to activate it. Inactivated, the desktop will be organized to focus on the application currently being used front and center, while other open windows organize neatly on the side.

The uses of Stage Manager:
1) Focusing on one app: When an application opens, it opens right in the center of your screen. All the rest of the applications slide to the side so that you can work on whatever you want without any kind of clutter.
2) Other Windows: To switch to another application or window, simply click on it from the side setup. It brings the window to the front, and hence, toggling between tasks becomes quite easy.
3) Customize Your Stage Manager Setup: Drag windows on and off the side to set how many apps show up in Stage Manager. And if you have several desktop or space, Stage Manager remembers your setup across your spaces.

Benefits Of Using Stage Manager:

1) Reduced Clutter: By organizing all of your windows and apps, Stage Manager helps you create a cleaner workspace. And the fewer windows to distract you, the better.

2) Improved Accessibility: All your regularly used applications are just a click away and hence no more difficulty in multitasking, which means better workflow surely.

MANAGING WINDOWS AND DESKTOPS ON YOUR IMAC WITH MISSION CONTROL

Mission Control is a powerful feature on macOS that extends your workspace by showing you all opened windows and handling multiple desktop spaces, also called "spaces." Mission Control gives you a quick glance at your applications; it keeps your workspace cleaned up and makes switching between applications easier. Mission Control lets you have multiple virtual desktops. Here's how you can use Mission Control and how to create and manage multiple desktops using it.

What Is Mission Control?

Mission Control shows all opened windows, split views, and spaces in one view. You can locate right away and switch to any application. Once you enter Mission Control all active windows show up in one layer so that you don't get lost in task switching.

Entering And Exiting Mission Control

You can turn on Mission Control the following ways:
1) Keyboard Shortcut:
   a) Press the F3 key - those three little rectangles at the top of your keyboard. It's usually labeled with the Mission Control icon.
   b) You can also hit Control + Up Arrow for Mission Control.
2) Trackpad Gesture: If you're using a MacBook or a trackpad, swipe up using 3 or 4 fingers upwards depending on how you have set up your trackpad, to enter Mission Control.
3) Dock Icon: You can also add the Mission Control icon to your Dock for quick access. To do so, first open your Mission Control, right-click the desired icon in the Dock, and select Options > Keep in Dock.

Using Mission Control
Immediately after entering Mission Control, you will see all the opened windows are arranged in one layer. Here's how to navigate and make full use of this feature:
1) Choose a Window: Clicking on any window brings it to the front and active. There is no need to minimize any of the windows or attempt to reach a window that may lie buried beneath.
2) Viewing Multiple Spaces: If you created any additional desktops, or spaces, those will be displayed, as well as the apps you're using in Split View. You can click the top of the Mission Control

screen on any of these thumbnails to jump immediately to that particular space.

3) Close or Rearrange Windows: You can also drag windows around in Mission Control to move them, or close them by hovering your cursor over the window and clicking the close button - the red dot.

CREATE AND MANAGE DESKTOP SPACES

If one desktop isn't sufficient to keep your work organized, you can create multiple desktop spaces using Mission Control. As a matter of fact, this is a great way of organizing your work across several projects or tasks.

Creating A New Desktop Space:

1) Enter Mission Control: Clicking the + icon, or by pressing Mission Control: If you followed the steps above to enter Mission Control.

2) Add a Space: Place your mouse cursor to the screen's top right-hand corner, and click the + button-this means "Add Desktop." This opens a new desktop space.

3) Name Your Spaces: By default, new spaces will be named "Desktop 1," "Desktop 2," etc. You can right-click on the space and Rename for more natural naming that is easier to identify in later steps.

Switching Between Spaces:

230

Once you have set up several, it becomes second nature to change between them using the following ways:

1) Keyboard Shortcuts: Control + Right Arrow and Control + Left Arrow keyboard shortcuts will enable you to flip between desktop spaces.
2) Mission Control: Just jump into Mission Control and then click at the top of the screen on which space you'd like to flip to.
3) Trackpad Gesture: With a trackpad, swipe left or right using three fingers to switch across spaces (you can also swipe with four fingers).

Moving Windows Between Spaces:

You can drag windows between other spaces to better arrange them:

1) Activate Mission Control.
2) Drag a Window: Click and drag the window of your choice to the top of your screen to your desired space by holding onto that window. Let go of the mouse to drop that window in that space.

DELETING SPACES

To delete any space you no longer need:

1) Go into Mission Control.
2) Hover Over the Space: Hover your cursor over the space which you want to delete. You will see an "X" appear in the corner of the thumbnail of the space.
3) Space Removal: Click the "X" to remove the space. Any open window in that space will move to another available space.

MISSION CONTROL-USAGE BENEFITS

1) Clarity and Focus: this feature allows you to operate multiple spaces and dedicate distinct screen portions to whatever is at hand, therefore reducing or completely avoiding diversion of attention.

2) Quick Access: through Mission Control, you'll get access to any opened application in the shortest time; this may save you from wasting much time in search of windows.

3) Organization of the workflow: Creating separate desktop spaces makes your workflow organized if you are working on multiple projects or more than one task simultaneously.

THE RED, YELLOW, AND GREEN BUTTONS

Red Button - Close Window

The red button mainly closes the current window of any application that you are using. However, the result for clicking this button can be different depending on the application you are working with:

1) Close Current Window: This only closes the current window in most of the applications. The application, however remains open and you can use it as you want. Using Safari, if you click on the button in red, the window of Safari will be closed

while the app stays opened and you may open another window or tab later.

2) Quit Application: For some applications - especially utilities or lighter programs - this red button will quit the whole application, therefore closing all windows. Examples of applications that would do this are TextEdit or Preview. For these programs, clicking the red button exits you completely out of the application. Tip: You can actually just quit an application without having to close the window by using Command + Q.

Yellow Button (Minimize Window)

The yellow button minimizes the current window, temporarily hiding its view. When you minimize a window, it slides down into the Dock on the right side.

1) Temporary Closure: The minimized window does not get closed; instead, it shrinks down to an icon in the Dock. This helps the user clear his/her desktop without losing work or the state of the application.

2) Restoring a Minimized Window: To open a minimized window, click the icon of the window in the Dock. The window opens to its previous size and to its previously set location.

Note: Press the Command + M keys to instantly minimize the currently active window.

Green Button for Full Screen and Split View

The green button has a number of functions, foremost among which is that it makes the window switch to full screen or allows for the activation of Split View thus enabling you to work with two windows side by side.

1) Full Screen: The green button opens the current window full screen, without seeing either the menu bar or the Dock. To exit full-screen mode, move your cursor to the top of your display and click the green button in the top-left corner again, or press Esc.

2) Split View: To work with two different applications side by side, click and hold the green button. This will bring up options to place the window either on the screen's left or right side. Once you have selected a side, you can choose another open window to fill in.

Note: For quick toggling between full-screen and windowed mode, double click the title bar of the window or use the key combination Control + Command + F.

Making The Most Of The Traffic Light Buttons

To fully utilize the traffic light buttons, then here are some things you could try doing:

1) Know the Application Behavior: At times, certain applications shut completely down when the red button is clicked. Many of them do not. Know what an app does, and that aids in workflow management.

2) Maintain Your Desktop: Use the yellow button to minimize windows instead of closing them. Keep your desktop organized; this helps you get to any application easily, without having to reopen it.

3) Split View for Multitasking: Use the green button to multitask in Split View. Perhaps you want to compose an email as you have a document open to your side; this is very helpful if you are doing research, writing, or need to have more than one application on at the same time.

4) Keyboard Shortcuts: Also, memorize the keyboard shortcuts for these actions: Command + W for close, Command + M for minimize, and Control + Command + F for full-screen to have smooth work and save your time.

CHAPTER 16: TAKING SCREENSHOTS OR SCREEN RECORDINGS ON AN IMAC

You can take screenshots of your screen or record your screen in a number of ways using your Mac. The Screenshot app is a free application pre-installed on your Mac, which has a suite of tools that allow you to easily capture screenshots or record your screen while giving you options to customize the capture with a timer delay or showing mouse pointer and clicks.

STEPS FOR SCREENSHOT / SCREEN RECORDINGS

STEP 1: OPEN SCREENSHOT

Press Shift-Command-5 on your keyboard. This will open the Screenshot interface-a set of tools at the bottom of your display. You could similarly open Screenshot from Launchpad.

STEP 2: SELECT YOUR TOOL

In the Screenshot panel, you'll see a series of icons for different capture options. Now select the tool that best describes what you want to do:

236

1) Capture Entire Screen [icon]: First icon clicks to take a screenshot of your entire display.

2) Capture a Window [icon]: Second icon clicks to capture a selected window. Just after choosing this option, you will be required to click at the window which you want to capture.

3) Capture a Portion of the Screen [icon]: In this context, with the third icon, you can shoot a selected area of the screen. You can click and drag on the frame to position and resize by dragging the edges.

4) Record Entire Screen [icon]: You can start recording your whole screen with the selection of the fourth icon. It may be helpful in creating tutorials or capturing gameplay.

5) Capture a Section of Screen [icon]- Below the section capture option, the fifth icon from the bottom will record just a part of the screen. To capture a part of the screen, you click and drag through the section you want to record.

STEP 3: USING SCREENSHOT AND SCREEN RECORDING OPTIONS

After opening the Screenshot tool using Shift-Command-5, you will see the **Options** pop-up menu, from where you will customize your

237

screenshot or screen recording. That menu gives you options for configuring what you want to capture to suit your needs and better organize the screenshots and recordings.

Accessing and Using Options

Once the Screenshot tool is opened, find the Options pop-up menu in the panel. Click on it, and you'll see a variety of options available that you can set. Which options appear depend on whether you're shooting a screenshot or recording a video.

Key Options Explained

1) **Save to**: Choose Where to Save the File.
   a) Location to Save: In the category of "**Save to**", you find that the locations are pre-set for either Desktop, Documents, or Clipboard. You can choose any of these regarding your convenience.
   b) Other Location: If you want to save your file in another folder, then select Other Location. This opens a file browser from which you can browse through your directories and select the exact folder you'd want the screenshot or recording to be saved. This is especially helpful for keeping your captures organized by projects or topics.

2) **Timer:** Set Up Delay.
The **Timer** will let you have the options of specifying how long to wait before capturing the screen. You

238

may have 5-second or 10-second options. By setting a timer, you take a few seconds to prepare your screen properly. An example would be if you want certain applications opened or windows placed for the shot or recording.

3) **Microphone:** Using a Microphone During a Screen Recording.
   a) Microphone Selection - If you are recording your screen and would like to include audio commentary, there is an option for selecting the **Microphone**. Within that option, you should be able to select the one you would like by simply left-clicking on it. Doing this will put a checkmark highlighting in your selected microphone, showing it is on.
   b) Disable Microphone: If you do not want to add audio to your recording, then you can select the option **None** from the microphone options. This option gives you an opportunity to focus solely on the visual features of your recording with no stress from noises or commentaries.

4) **Show Floating Thumbnail:**
   a) Whenever the capture of a screenshot or the beginning of a recording takes place, it will float as a thumbnail for some time in the bottom-right corner of your screen. It will give you immediate access to the captured image or recorded video to work on it before it gets saved automatically into your specified location.

b) Floating Thumbnail Options
   i) To activate the floating thumbnail, click on the menu for **Options → Show Floating Thumbnail**. A checkmark will appear beside the option, indicating it is activated.
   ii) To display the floating thumbnail, check that box. Click the option again to turn off the display of the floating thumbnail; the checkmark is removed. You might want to do this if you find the thumbnail annoying or if you don't have any particular need to have immediate access to the capture.

5) **Remember Last Selection**:
   a) Every time you capture a particular area of your screen by selecting that area, Screenshot offers you an option to save that area for captures afterwards. It does this for repetitive tasks where you constantly have to capture the same part of your screen over and over.
   b) Enable **Remember Last Selection**: Check the box beside Remember Last Selection found on the Options menu in order to allow the image to remember your last selection. A checked box indicates that this is already enabled. With this on, when next you open the Screenshot tool, it will already pre-set the capture area to the area dimensions you previously used by default, and you can have it streamlined.

c) The feature can be disabled by clicking on **Remember Last Selection** again; it will remove the checkmark. In such a way, settings will be automatically reset on the next capture.

6) **Show Mouse Pointer**:
   a) The Mouse Pointer: You may also want to capture the mouse pointer while you take screenshots to add context or to highlight a certain screen area. This is useful in tutorial materials, for example, or other similar types of presentations.
   b) Show Mouse Pointer: If you want to capture a mouse pointer, then after clicking on the Options menu, check Show Mouse Pointer. You will notice that this option has a checkmark to its side once its enabled, therefore in all your captures, the pointer will appear.
   c) Disable Mouse Pointer: If you do not want the mouse pointer to appear in your screenshots, just click Show Mouse Pointer again to clear the check box. It will exclude the pointer in all your future captures.

STEP 4: START THE SCREENSHOT/SCREEN RECORDING

Once you have set up the Screenshot tool and selected your options, it's time to start the actual capture or recording process. This step is very important because it assists you in getting what you want with a lot of efficiency.

Depending on your preference for capture - whether for the whole screen or part of it, or a window - you do the following:

1) For the Whole Screen or Part of It: Once you have selected an area, or chosen option for capturing the whole screen, click on the **Capture** button inside the Screenshot tool panel. Immediately, a screenshot of the selected area will be taken.

2) For a Window: To capture a window, position your cursor over the window you want to record; click on the window when the pointer is at the appropriate location. You can use this to capture clear backgrounds for only the selected window.

3) For Screen Recordings: To capture a recording of your screen, select Record from the Screenshot tool. This will immediately open a recording session in the Sorter window. To stop your recording, simply select the Stop button ⊙ from the menu bar at the top of your screen. This way it is quick and easy to stop recording without returning to the Screenshot selection tool.

STEP 5: INTERACTING WITH THE FLOATING THUMBNAIL

If you've switched on the Show Floating Thumbnail option, immediately after snapping a screenshot or starting a recording, you will briefly see a thumbnail of your capture pop up in the bottom right corner of the screen. On that thumbnail you can do the following:

1) Swipe right to save: You can save the screenshot or recording quickly by swiping the thumbnail to the right; this will immediately save the file to the location you've identified and dismiss the thumbnail, saving extra work.
2) Drag the Thumbnail: If you would like to use the captured material in other applications, you can drag the thumbnail to a document, email, note, or Finder window. That saves several steps and really makes your screenshot or recording a part of your project.
3) Click the Thumbnail: Click the floating thumbnail to open a dedicated window where you can engage with your capture. In the window, options include:
   a) Mark up screenshot - just annotate or highlight part of your screenshot using the built - in markup tools to make it useful for tutorials, presentations, or feedback.
   b) Trim Recording: When recording, be it video or screen, use the trim in the front or the back to get rid of extra video besides what is important to help ensure your final product is of higher quality.
   c) Share the Screenshot or Recording: The window actions on this matter include sharing options. You can directly forward the file via email, messages, or other sharing platforms without saving first.

APP INTEGRATION AND SAVING

Depending on what app you have chosen to save to, an application will automatically open once your screenshot or recording is saved. For instance, if you chose to save it to an application such as Preview or Photos, that actual application opens and you can view or edit the content that you have captured immediately. This may fit more neatly into a workflow and make managing your screenshots and recordings easier.

TAKING SCREENSHOTS WITH KEYBOARD SHORTCUTS

Taking screenshots on an iMac using keyboard shortcuts is fast and efficient. You can take images of your screen without having to use menus. Screenshots via a keyboard shortcut appear directly on your desktop, where you easily access and manage them. Accordingly, the following options, or shortcuts, are available in capturing your screen in various ways:

General Tips for Using Keyboard Shortcuts

If you want to copy a screenshot to the clipboard so you can paste it directly into an application - say, an email or document-then press the Control key along with the other keys. For instance, to copy the entire screen, you would press Control-Shift-Command-3.

Screenshot Actions And Their Shortcuts

1) Capture the Entire Screen:
   a) Shortcut: Shift-Command-3.
   b) This command captures a screenshot of your entire display and saves the file to your desktop.
2) Capture a Portion of the Screen:
   a) Shortcut: Press Shift-Command-4.
   b) After pressing this command, a crosshair pointer will appear. With the crosshair pointing to the beginning of the section you like to screenshot, click the mouse or trackpad button, hold and drag over what you want to capture, and then release the button, which captures the shot.
3) Shoot a single Window or capture the Menu Bar:
   a) Shortcut: Press Shift-Command-4, then press the Space bar.
   b) This will change your pointer to a camera. Move the camera pointer over the window or menu bar you want to capture; as you hover over, the area will be highlighted. Click on the highlighted area for the screenshot.
4) Screenshot a Menu and/or Menu Items:
   a) Shortcut: Open the menu you want, then press Shift-Command-4.
   b) With this command, drag the pointer over the items to capture them from a menu. This is useful if you want to capture a contextual menu or some drop-down for documentation or tutorial purposes.
5) Open Screenshot Utility:

a) Shortcut: Shift-Command-5 (⇧⌘5)
b) This opens the Screenshot utility, which shows options for capturing different areas of the screen and screen recordings. This utility offers extra settings related to the capture and saving.
6) Capture the Touch Bar:
a) Shortcut: Shift-Command-6 (⇧⌘6).
b) If your Mac comes with a Touch Bar, then this captures what's currently inside the Touch Bar.

MANAGING YOUR SCREENSHOTS

By default, screenshots are saved as image files to your desktop after being taken. Here is how you might manage them more effectively:

1) Format of the Files: Generally, the screenshots are saved in PNG format since it gives a good balance between quality and file size. However, if you want any other format, you can convert them using any of several image editors.

2) Organization: You would want to create a specific screenshot folder so that it would not clutter up your desktop. You can then transfer your screenshot files there for better organization.

3) Screenshot editing: You can open it in Preview or any other photo editing tool to edit the screenshot. This becomes helpful when you want to annotate the screenshot or place text or shapes onto the screenshots to highlight something in a presentation or documentation.

4) Screenshot Sharing: You can share your screenshots in email, messaging apps, or even

cloud storage by simple drag-and-drop from desktop to target application or upload via Google Drive/Dropbox, among others.

CUSTOMIZING KEYBOARD SHORTCUTS FOR SCREENSHOTS

To alter the default keyboard shortcuts for taking screenshots on an iMac, pursue the subsequent procedure:

1. System Settings: Click the Apple menu, at the top-left corner of your screen. Then select **System Settings.**

2. Set up Keyboard Preferences: In the System Settings sidebar, click Keyboard ⌨. This area has several options that allow you to personalize your keyboard and hotkeys.

3. Open Keyboard Shortcuts: After opening Keyboard preferences, find the Keyboard Shortcuts option and click on it. You will now see categories of different types of keyboard shortcuts that are available on your Mac.

4. 4.Choose Screenshots: Within the categories list, find where it says Screenshots, then click to open this option to show what keys are currently assigned as keyboard shortcuts for taking screenshots.

5. Change Shortcuts:
   a) Here you will see the list of default shortcuts for actions like capture whole screen, capturing a selected portion, and so on. To change any

shortcut, first click on the existing shortcut followed by pressing the new key combination which you want to assign it. Make sure that the new combination does interfere with the other already present shortcuts.

b) To restore a default shortcut, this can usually be done by clicking a reset button or by re-entering the original shortcut.

6. Closing System Settings: Once you have made your desired changes, close the System Settings window. Your new shortcuts will be in effect immediately.

SCREENSHOT AND SCREEN RECORD FILE FORMATS

When you capture screenshots and recordings on your iMac, they are saved in the following file formats:

1. Screenshots: These will be exported in .png format. The .png file format has very good lossless image compression. This file format is quite well-suited to keep your screenshot clear, especially for detailed content.

2. Screen Recordings: These will be exported in .mov format. MOV is a versatile format to record video that allows good quality while being compatible with a wide range of players.

FILE NAMING CONVENTIONS

The filenames for your screenshot and screen recording are in a standardized format, which starts either with "Screenshot" or "Screen Recording, " followed by the date and time of capture. This naming convention assists users in recognizing quickly when the screenshot or recording was taken to help in file organization and finding later. A good example would be a screenshot taken on October 25, 2024, at 3:15 PM; it would be named something like "Screenshot 2024-10-25 at 15.15.00.png".

LIMITATIONS ON TAKING SCREENSHOTS

However easy the process is on an iMac, here are a few of the limitations:

1. Certain Applications: You may find some application-specific restrictions to capture the screenshots of the system. For example, screenshotting applications like DVD Player or any content that is kept under Digital Rights Management will likely be restricted. It usually comes into action to prevent copyright issues and sensitive material security.

2. Overlays and Pop-ups: Overlays or pop-ups in applications are not recognized because some may be designed active, or their appearance does not coincide with the syntax that is needed for a screenshot to recognize them.

INDEX

T

Made in the USA
Las Vegas, NV
22 February 2025

18546079R00144